Television Weathercasting

Television
Weathercasting:
A History

by
Robert Henson

McFarland & Company, Inc., Publishers
Jefferson, North Carolina, and London

British Library Cataloguing-in-Publication data are available

Library of Congress Cataloguing-in-Publication Data

Henson, Robert, 1960–
    Television weathercasting : a history / by Robert Henson.
      p. cm.
    [Includes index.]
    Includes bibliographical references.
    ISBN 0-89950-492-2 (lib. bdg. : 50# alk. paper) ∞
    1. Television weathercasting—United States—History.
  2. Television weathercasters—United States. I. Title.
QC877.5.H46 1990
551.6′309—dc20   89-43696
                                            CIP

Manufactured in the United States of America

McFarland & Company, Inc., Publishers
  Box 611, Jefferson, North Carolina 28640

To my parents and friends

Contents

Preface

Growing up in Tornado Alley, one learns to appreciate television weather. I was a child of seven when I first came under the spell of weathercasting. It was a muggy spring night in Oklahoma, and as usual, thunderstorms were approaching. As I sat watching one of those especially mindless situation comedies peculiar to the 1960s, the show was interrupted by a serious young woman talking about tornadoes.

How does she know what the weather's doing? I wondered. The way Lola Hall described terrifying storms with such calmness and authority carried a touch of magic for me. From that night on, I was hooked on meteorology—and on the way television and weather interacted.

That fascination has held firm. Television weather shows are still an anchor of my life, something I rarely go without for even a day. While most people don't share my degree of interest, there is an ever-present demand by the general public for weather information.

Few have taken close note of this phenomenon. In 1986, when I first thought of writing this book, I was appalled to find that television weather was all but ignored as a subject of serious inquiry. Books on television news and sports lined the shelves, but there were none on television weather. Major dictionaries included *newscast* and *sportscast* but not *weathercast*. Didn't weather affect more people more directly than economic summits or baseball games?

In this atmosphere of neglect, my work was cut out for me. Writing this book was thus a matter of piecing together scattered articles, book passages, interviews, and personal recollections. Although there is a lot of information here, this certainly isn't the whole story. I offer my regrets in advance for those incidents, programs, and people that were omitted. This volume is presented not as the final word on weathercasting but as only one snapshot of a work in progress, being updated throughout the country in television studios large and small. (Readers should note that all station affiliations given for weathercasters in this book were current as of this writing but are always subject to change. Also, most television stations include the suffix -TV with their call letters, such as WRC-TV. In the interest of simplicity, I've deleted the suffix unless needed for clarity.)

Most books, including this one, couldn't be accurately written without the help of many people. My warm thanks go to the dozens of weathercasters I interviewed over the past three years. Almost without exception, these people were gracious and generous with their time. Many of them took the effort to send me anecdotes, pictures, and other firsthand material documenting their work. These contributions and others are acknowledged elsewhere in the book.

My late parents, Charles Franklin and Bettie Thomas Henson, gave me the loving encouragement and free reins every child should have. To them, and to everyone who feels a special affinity with the weather, I dedicate this book.

Acknowledgments

Reference librarians are among my world's unsung heroes. I owe a great debt to the employees that guided my search through the stacks for hidden nuggets of background on television weather at the University of Oklahoma's Bizzell Library, the University of Colorado's Norlin Library, the Denver Public Library, and the Library of Congress. Special gratitude goes to Karen Livesy of the National Association of Broadcasters (NAB) Library and to Catharine Heinz, George Franchois, and Luisa Llacuna of the Broadcast Pioneers Library at NAB. Both facilities are gold mines of information on the electronic media.

Several companies in the television weather field were kind enough to give me leads, information, and photos. Thanks go to Eva Moreland and Ray Ban at The Weather Channel; Doug Hinahara at ColorGraphics Systems, Inc.; John Carlson at Alden Electronics, Inc.; and Peter Leavitt of WSI Corporation.

Of the many weathercasters whom I interviewed, a few were especially interested in this project and happy to help out. Among those who contributed beyond the call of duty were George Winterling, Jim Fidler, Jack Capell, Valerie Voss, Don Woods, June Bacon-Bercey, Jim Williams, Joe Witte, Nash Roberts, Bob Lynott, Joel Bartlett, and Kirk Melhuish. Special thanks are due to Bob Ryan and Harry Spohn, who allowed a friendly stranger to document their weathercasting for Chapter 2. (Peggy Lamson's *Stay Tuned* was the inspiration for that section of the book.) I would be remiss in not mentioning the publicity departments of the stations I contacted; many of the photos in this book were supplied through their courtesy.

It was while hunting for a master's thesis topic at the University of Oklahoma that I conceived of writing this book. For fear of leaving one out, I won't list all the colleagues and professors that gave me support in the

Oklahoma meteorology and journalism schools. I hope they'll accept this collective acknowledgment.

Though it can be painful to have one's work examined critically, there is no substitute for a good reviewer. I had several, including Matt Kelsch, Michelle Layfield, Ken Heideman, Verna Watterson, Art Tarr, and Denice Walker. Barney Gibbs was a diligent long-distance checker of facts on short notice. At the National Weather Service's Office of Constituent Affairs, Walt Cottrell and Ed Gross provided helpful feedback on Chapter 4 after having guided me through the NWS weathercasting files during my research.

1

"And Now, the Forecast..."

- A burly, middle-aged man wearing high heels and a feathered headdress issues birthday greetings to a 102-year-old Hoosier.
- A frantic newscaster warns of a mile-wide tornado approaching town, beseeching viewers to take cover.
- A Lhasa apso pants and wags his tail while an announcer reads tomorrow's outlook.

What do these wildly differing scenes have in common? All three illustrate the ways television provides weather information to the United States.

Weathercasting is as American as football, the product of a large and mobile nation plugged into mass media and blessed (or cursed) with hundreds of different climatic regimes. From the turn of this century when weather forecasting began to mature, the "weatherman" slowly became a trusted yet sometimes scorned symbol. This process intensified when television gave a face to the weather, replacing the never-seen government forecaster in his office with a very public entertainer-weatherperson.

Television weather has since earned its place as a distinctive archetype in United States culture. A radical political group of the 1960s named themselves the Weathermen. Pop music has had the Weather Girls. Countless comedy acts have satirized the part of the newscast that itself pokes fun at almost everything sacred.

Is the weather really that important, compared to bombings and Super Bowls? Survey after survey shows it is. Despite the attention heaped on news and sports anchors, it's weather that consistently ranks as the top draw in both local and national news (when featured in the latter). Viewers of Los Angeles' KABC have chosen weather as their favorite news subject over crime, Hollywood, and 15 other topics.[1] Five stations polled by the

1

National Weather Service in 1980 were unanimous in naming weather "the major reason that people watch the news program."[2]

There's more to the popularity of television weather than the information it presents. Weathercasters are often celebrities on their home turf. A survey in the nation's top 50 television markets* found that weathercasters were rated above their news and sports counterparts for awareness and appeal.[3] Willard Scott, the jovial weathercaster of NBC's "Today," drew over 27,000 supportive phone calls when the newspaper *USA Today* asked its readers whether Scott was helping or hindering the show.[4]

Unlike many other topics appearing in the daily news, weather is universally tangible. It's right outside the window every second of every day. That presence, mixed with the constant change and variety of day-to-day weather events, makes tomorrow's forecast one of the most important elements in local news. And when disruptive weather hits — when tornadoes or snowstorms strike — weather can all but dominate television news for days on end.

Of course, dry facts alone aren't enough to attract audiences in the flashy world of television. Weathercasters have to present their information with liveliness, or at least friendliness. In searching for the magic blend of science and show biz that keeps viewers coming back, stations have gone to absurd lengths. What serious newscaster would be asked to read the day's headlines while submerged in a tank of water, as Ginger Stanley did for the CBS "Morning Show" weather in 1957?[5] Would even the best-paid sportscaster in America report to duty dressed as Carmen Miranda, as Willard Scott once did?[6]

These stunts have, for better or worse, tied weathercasting to frivolity in the eyes of many. Yet the job has its deadly serious side. Weather anchors in Tornado Alley stay up all night during storm season, doggedly watching radar screens and warning the public of life-threatening twisters. News and weather reporters travel thousands of miles each year to cover hurricanes threatening the United States. Seldom does television aid the public in such a direct, unselfish fashion.

In the process of watching weathercasters, Americans have learned something about weather itself. Seeing a cold front march across the United States over a week's time makes clear the connection between record heat one day and biting chill the next. And as public weather savvy has increased, so have the tools of the television weather trade. A dizzying array of charts, graphs, and displays now lie at the disposal of weatherpeople. In the hands of a skilled weathercaster, this complex technology can bring

Market is the technical term among broadcasters for the population in a geographical area dominated by those television stations based in a specific city. The United States included 212 such markets in 1988.

clarity, simplifying the vast processes underlying world climate and giving one the sense that weather makes sense.

THE BEGINNINGS OF WEATHER NEWS

Television weather evolved from a long-standing tradition of weather reporting, a legacy going back to the personal records kept by colonial weather observers. Presidents George Washington and Thomas Jefferson were both avid weather followers, recording sky and wind data at least twice daily for periods of years. Jefferson duly noted the temperature of 72.5 degrees in Philadelphia at 1:00 PM on July 4, 1776, the day he and others signed the Declaration of Independence. Washington kept meticulous records until the day before he died.[7]

Storms also drew the interest of early weather observers, just as they do today. Among the earliest published accounts of weather was a report from one British weekly in the 1650s of a severe rainstorm (scooping the competition).[8] But such pioneering weather reports left much to be desired; the process of compiling data at a central point to analyze storm progress had not been established. Even as long-distance communication improved in the late 1800s, a major storm could still go unreported beyond its area of impact. A huge gale on New Year's Day 1895 killed some 400 people in ships off the British coast, but the event failed to make London papers for days.[9]

In the United States, sporadic weather coverage in almanacs of the colonial era improved with the advent of "penny papers" in the 1830s. As the first news publication aimed at a mass audience, they emphasized concrete events (like weather) over abstract political discussions.[10] Still, weather was hardly a staple of the newspapers' editorial diet; as late as 1860, the *New York Times* carried no regular weather feature.

It was the formation of the National Weather Service in 1870 that paved the way for routine weather coverage in newspapers, and later in radio and television.* Compiling telegraph data from across the growing nation, the Weather Service issued reports and "indications" (forecasts), and distributed these daily to newspapers. Within five years of the service's formation, the *New York Times* carried several column inches daily devoted to "The Weather," with a summary of the previous day's conditions and forecasts for states in the Northeast.

The "new journalism" of the 1880s further emphasized reader service, and weather news became even more prominent. Joseph Pulitzer's *New York World* founded the traditional weather "ear" at the upper-right-hand

---

*Throughout this book, "National Weather *Service*" and "U.S. Weather *Bureau*" are used to describe the same agency at various points in its history. See Chapter 3 for a full explanation.

corner of the front page, giving the next day's forecast.[11] By 1900, the *New York Times* had followed suit with a front page box giving forecasts and instructing readers to turn inside for more details.

Despite the havoc it wreaked, World War I provided a major step forward in weather forecasting and weather news treatment. Vilhelm Bjerknes, a Scandinavian military meteorologist, discovered the presence of moving boundaries that separated warm and cold air masses. Using a wartime analogy, he labeled the boundaries "fronts" and developed a comprehensive theory of their behavior.[12] The discovery improved forecasts dramatically while adding a new element to the vocabulary of weather news. In the 1920s, many United States papers began printing weather maps, complete with fronts, substantially increasing the space devoted to weather.

WIRELESS WEATHER

Meanwhile, radio was entering the United States household. In 1900, the Weather Bureau subsidized an experiment to test whether sending vocalized messages by radio was feasible. Weather stayed on the front line of early programming as experimental stations at colleges and civic centers transmitted weather as early as 1919. However, these first efforts were scattered and sporadic; radio wasn't yet accepted as the proper means of transmitting important news.

It took President Franklin Roosevelt and the New Deal to make weather a standard part of radio. Under FDR, the Weather Bureau stepped up its involvement with radio stations, forging a set of links between local broadcasters and local Weather Bureau personnel. Radio listeners of the late 1930s heard weather incorporated in the burgeoning news programs of the day, and the subject occasionally got its own daily 15-minute spot.

Even in this nonvisual medium, the seeds of television weather were being planted. Some stations simply assigned the weather to an anchor, who might or might not have added life to the statistics. But in a few cities, there was the "weatherman," specifically designed to lend a touch of character and authority to the forecast. Such was the case with Jim Fidler, a young scientist fresh out of Ball State University, who began doing weather in 1934 for WLBC in Muncie, Indiana. A typical Fidler broadcast began like this:

> "By telephone, telegraph, teletype, radio and the mail, WLBC's own meteorologist, Jimmie Fidler, 'radio's original weatherman,' gathers the information on the weather as it is and as it is to be. Now, here is Jimmie with his maze of weather data that he will unravel into a simple and complete picture of the weather."

A SCIENTIFIC APPROACH THROUGH POPULAR APPEAL • • • • • • •

THE LATEST FORECAST, COMPLETE CORRECT
INFORMATION, MOST COMPREHENSIVE OUTLOOK
IN OTHER WORDS—
THE ENTIRE STORY OF THE WEATHER
AS IT IS DONE IN A TEN MINUTE UP TO THE MINUTE
WEATHER BROADCAST

IN A VERY ENTERTAINING FASHION JIMMIE TELLS
HOW HE GATHERS THE DATA, PREPARES THE
MAPS, AND READS THEM TO HIS LISTENERS SO
THAT THEY ENJOY THEM AND LEARN.

DO YOU ENJOY KNOWING ABOUT THE WEATHER?
THE LISTENER WRITES:
THE FARMER—
"WE PLAN OUR WORK BY YOUR REPORTS"
THE TRUCKER:
"YOU HAVE SAVED US MANY DOLLARS"
THE BUILDER:
"DID JIMMIE SAY IT WOULD BE OK TO POUR—TODAY"
HOUSEWIVES:
"I'M GOING TO WASH TOMORROW—
JIMMIE SAID THE SUN WILL SHINE."

OFFICIALLY JIMMIE IS KNOWN AS·
JAMES C. FIDLER
CO-OPERATIVE OBSERVER
U. S..WEATHER BUREAU

Jimmie Fidler
"RADIO'S ORIGINAL
WEATHERMAN"
(COPYRIGHT)
ORIGINATOR OF POPULAR BROADCASTS
OF AUTHENTIC WEATHER INFORMATION

This 1934 brochure promoted the radio weathercasts of Jim Fidler, who had just begun at station WLBC in Muncie, Indiana. Fidler was among the first to see weather broadcasting as a chance to expand on Weather Bureau reports. (Courtesy Jim Fidler)

Fidler's show was the essence of down-to-earth weather reporting, complete and accurate yet uncluttered with jargon:

> "Good afternoon. Here is the U.S. Weather Bureau forecast for the eastern part of the U.S. The outlook is for increasing cloudiness over most of the New England states and with rising temperatures over the Central Atlantic states tonight and Saturday...."[13]

A hint of what would soon happen to weather news came in 1940 and 1941 when a handful of experimental television stations began broadcasting. Weather made its debut on Cincinnati television with Jim Fidler, who used a format similar to that of his radio show. But other experimental weather shows appeared on the few television sets in existence, mostly in the Northeast, and these programs pointed to a changing approach.

New York City's first television weathercast appeared October 14, 1941, on the experimental outlet WNBT (later to become WNBC). The star was none other than Wooly Lamb, an animated creature that remained on WNBT for seven years. Wooly introduced each program by looking skyward with a telescope, then faced viewers to sing:

"It's hot, it's cold. It's rain, it's fair. It's all mixed up together. But I, as
Botany's wooly lamb, predict tomorrow's weather."

After Wooly's exit, a slide showing the next day's forecast was
displayed. ("Botany" referred to Botany Wrinkle-Proof ties, the sponsor.)[14]

Perhaps it struck nobody as odd that an innocuous lamb was chosen
to announce events that greatly affect life and property. In any case, Wooly
Lamb was a harbinger of weather's eventual segregation from other television news. World War II postponed the further expansion of television for
a few years, but television weather now had its first role model.

WEATHERCASTING TAKES OFF

Following World War II, television emerged from its experimental phase
with remarkable speed. The number of sets in use skyrocketed to 3.6
million in 1949 and 9.7 million in 1950 (even greater growth was to follow).[15] A total of 69 television stations were on the air in 1949; these were
located across the United States instead of being clustered in the urban
Northeast as were the experimental stations of 1940–1941.[16]

With almost 20 years of traumatic world events behind them, the
American public of the late 1940s took their news seriously. Weather was
no exception since radio had generally treated weather as a subset of the
news at large. "The first training for a new man in our newsroom is learning
to write the weather story," said one radio news director in 1946.[17] Some
radio stations used meteorologists from the Weather Bureau or even hired
their own. In short, weather news on radio was delivered with respect.

It was perhaps unavoidable that television weather would depart from
its radio roots. The visual nature of television demanded "action" in the
form of weather maps and bright, attractive people who could explain
them. The frontal theory of weather forecasting was then just 30 years old;
weather maps had become a newspaper standby, but the workings of occluded fronts and high-pressure ridges were hardly common knowledge.
Looking back at his early days, weathercasting pioneer Louis Allen took
note of the gap in public awareness:

"When I started out, the 'high' and the 'low' and the 'fronts' really meant
nothing. It was all part of the scientific jargon."[18]

With this lack of knowledge in mind, early television stations often
looked for weathercasters who were not necessarily polished announcers —

after all, the medium itself was still unpolished — but who did know something about weather. As it happened, a bumper crop of such people had just emerged from World War II. The war effort had trained thousands of enlisted men in meteorology, many of whom came back ready to use their knowledge in civilian life. Dozens of these veterans showed up on local weather programs in the late 1940s.

Washington, D.C., got its first television weather in 1948 from Louis Allen, who combined a drive to educate the public with an easygoing delivery. Allen's meteorological background came from service in the navy; he was among the forecasters of sea and swell conditions for the pivotal United States invasions of Iwo Jima and Okinawa.[19]

While Allen and his contemporaries brought weather to local television, John Clinton Youle was the first to take it nationwide. Youle debuted with John Cameron Swayze's "Camel News Caravan" on NBC in 1949. His background as an air force weatherman and a writer-editor for NBC proved ideal for the task.[20] Still, as many who followed him were to learn, no weathercaster is immune to public ribbing. In this exchange from December 1949, Youle is introduced by reporter Cliff Utley, who had just interviewed Otis Hewitt of the Burlington, Iowa, Liars' Club:

UTLEY: Now, here's my colleague, Clint Youle, the NBC weatherman, whose predictions ... well, Otis, you might consider Clint for membership in your club sometime!

YOULE: Cliff, I hardly know whether to be flattered or chagrined at that sort of introduction.[21]

Youle and Allen's relaxed approaches were about as lighthearted as the earliest television weathercasts got. The influx of military men doing weather, some of them untrained in public speaking, gave much television weather of the late 1940s and early 1950s a serious, formal tone. Oklahoma City's WKY inaugurated its weather programming in 1950 with a sergeant from nearby Tinker Air Force Base whose comments were limited to a rehashing of the air force outlook. "It was pretty deadly stuff," wrote an observer years later.[22]

The days of straightforward weathercasting lasted longer than they might have, thanks to governmental fiat. Worried about the rapid proliferation of television stations clogging limited frequencies, the Federal Communications Commission put a freeze on station licensing from 1948 to 1952. This left the majority of United States cities with only one television station during the freeze period. With no competitors to spur new approaches to weathercasting, those stations already in place were inclined to keep whatever format they had already devised. If some of those early styles now seem dry and pedantic, they were impressive in their devotion to presenting weather with no frills attached.

THE PRANKSTERS ARRIVE

Public affection for television blossomed in the early 1950s, despite the FCC's freeze. Some 21.8 million sets were in use by 1952.[23] The first nationwide hit shows were drawing huge audiences. Networks were expanding their reach, acquiring station affiliates across the country and assembling slates of daily and weekly programs. Clearly, the infant medium was growing up.

Once the FCC freeze was lifted, applications for station licenses skyrocketed. The number of stations on the air grew from 108 to 469 in the first three post-freeze years (1952–1955).[24] Most cities with populations over 100,000 had at least two stations competing for viewers by the mid-1950s. The ratings race was now under way, and television weather was not to escape its effects.

Polish, appearance, and gimmicks became important tools in the newly competitive world of local television. If television was home entertainment, then surely even newscasts could be made entertaining. There were obvious constraints on the news itself (fires and shootings were hardly the stuff of humor), so weather evolved into a primary arena for making the news more palatable.

The result was television weather's wildest, most uninhibited period, the age of puppets, costumes, and "weathergirls." Practically anything and everything was tried to boost viewership. To note just two of the gimmicks used to present television weather in the mid-1950s:

- A Nashville weathercaster gave his forecast in verse (for example, "Rain today and rain tonight / Tomorrow still more rain in sight").[25]
- Viewers in New York could get weather information at midnight from an ostensibly sleepy woman in a short nightgown, tucking herself into bed.[26]

These methods of enlivening the weathercast had surprisingly little impact on the material presented, since most data and forecasts were taken directly from the National Weather Service (see Chapter 3). The familiar weathercast sequence—consisting of current weather conditions, previous highs and lows, current map, forecast map, and local forecast—was already well established; it carried such strong inherent logic that only the most daring of programmers altered it. Still, humorous goings-on were all too capable of detracting from important weather information or pushing it from the weathercast altogether.

Ironically, weathercasting as comic relief hit its apex in the mid-1950s, just as real progress was being made in meteorology. Radar scopes could now pinpoint severe thunderstorms and even some tornadoes; "hurricane-hunter" planes retrieved valuable data that improved warnings; jet-stream analysis and computer forecasting models were coming into use. However, in most weathercasts of the era, these scientific advances were buried under the sheer weight of jokes and gags.

RETURN OF THE PROFESSIONALS

Stepping in to quell the newly comic trend of television weather was the nation's foremost group of atmospheric scientists, the American Meteorological Society (AMS). Founded in 1919, the AMS included several thousand scholars, government forecasters, and others taking a serious interest in weather. Radio's treatment of weather in the pre-television era had drawn little complaint from the AMS; in fact, articles in the group's monthly journal had noted the potential benefits of mass distribution of weather data. However, by the mid-1950s, television weather had strayed far enough from its businesslike roots in radio to alarm the AMS hierarchy.

The society's response was to create an AMS seal of approval, to be conferred on weathercasters whose work met society guidelines for completeness, clarity, and professionalism. Plans for the seal were suggested in 1954 and approved in a May 1955 meeting of the AMS Council.[27] Word of the AMS plans reached the public in a *TV Guide* article of July 1955, bluntly titled "Weather Is No Laughing Matter." Author Francis Davis, a physics professor and pioneer in radio and television weather, summarized the AMS position.

> If TV weathermen are going to pose as experts, we feel they *should* be experts. We think the weather should be discussed with dignity. Dignity, not dullness. We think many TV "weathermen" make a caricature of what is essentially a serious and scientific occupation, help foster the notion that forecasters merely grab forecasts out of a fish bowl.[28]

Pointed as the AMS criticisms were, they had little initial impact on the tide of humor engulfing television weather. The late 1950s saw a continuation of lighthearted weather segments across the United States, while the AMS struggled to put together its seal-of-approval protocol. Newspapers and magazines covered the AMS efforts but took the opportunity to highlight the latest gimmicks. *Newsweek* looked at "Tricky Weather" in 1957, noting a puppet on St. Louis television, a "weather lion" in New York, and Bill Williams, the Nashville poet-weathercaster.[29]

Among the few weathercasters keeping a serious approach in the 1950s was Jim Fidler, shown in 1954 at WLWT, Cincinnati. (Courtesy Jim Fidler)

It was two more years before the AMS seal program finally began, with the first six seals awarded to those members who had collaborated in drawing up seal requirements. As laid out in the society's bulletin of February 1959, seal requirements were as follows: Interested weathercasters had to submit a written application and a film clip of one representative weathercast. These were reviewed by the AMS Radio-TV Committee, and the sample weathercast was graded by each member on informational value, educational value, audience interest, and professional attitude. Meanwhile, several AMS members from the applicant's viewing area were recruited to observe weathercasts secretly, looking for any lapses in taste or accuracy. If all these hurdles were cleared, the applicant received a seal of approval, along with the right to display it before or after all weathercasts. Radio-weather anchors could obtain a similar seal through a parallel process.[30]

The AMS seals made an immediate mark on the broadcast community. Seal holders' numbers grew slowly through the early 1960s, with 46 television weathercasters certified by 1964. Most of these were in large cities along the midwestern and northeastern urban corridors, with a few scattered across the southern plains and Gulf Coast.[31] While such small numbers hardly made a dent in the national weathercaster total, the AMS influence was greater than that count might indicate. As early as 1959, *TV Guide* observed that gimmicky weathercasting was on the wane.

> Today, there's less intentional humor in the weather forecasts we see on television ... but we are getting more factual information. In the past 10 years alone, television weathercasts have matured from off-the-cuff reading of the official weather bureau reports by announcers or pretty girls to serious interpretations of the official forecasts by either station meteorologists or announcers with weather training.[32]

Societal factors began to enhance this shift toward seriousness in the mid-1960s as the Vietnam War and domestic turmoil intensified. Flippant weathercasts did not blend well with these sobering news events. However, the few people who maintained a comic approach, like Willard Scott on Washington's WRC, became even more flamboyant. These weathercasts heralded a reaction to the staid, serious approach, a shift that would affect television news in general.

"HAPPY WEATHER"

While the AMS seal vastly improved the status of serious weathercasters, it hardly sounded the death knell for comics. A pervasive format known as "happy news" entered local television during the 1970s. The happy-news approach drastically altered local news and weather in ways still felt after nearly two decades.

Newscast structure was one visible change. In most markets during the 1950s and 1960s, weather had been isolated from news and sports reporting by commercial breaks, with no interaction between the three anchors. Often the segments were listed as separate programs, each with a different sponsor. Happy-news approaches melded the segments into a unified half-hour or hour show. Moreover, the news "team" was now instructed to make conversation that bridged the gaps between segments. The idea was to further an impression of newscasters as family (or at least close friends) concerned with one another's lives. Joking weatherpersons suited such a format well, resulting in a resurgence in humorous weather from its lull in popularity during the 1960s.

Paul Joseph, of Milwaukee's WTMJ, was an early recipient of the American Meteorological Society's seal of approval. His weather map in the early 1970s featured isobars and air-mass identification symbols. (Courtesy WTMJ)

Virtually all local newscasts had adopted some type of happy-news structure by the late 1970s, largely due to nationwide consulting firms that packaged and sold newscast formats, complete with introductory jingles and weather sets. Under these predeveloped formats, weathercasters typically received the same time—two to four minutes—they were allotted before. However, the required interaction between weatherpeople and other newscasters now consumed up to a minute of that time. Some cities opted for an hour or even 90 minutes of news, in which several brief weather segments were scattered. These, though, were often rehashes of the first weathercast, simply repeated for viewers tuning in late.

SERIOUS WEATHER MAKES A COMEBACK

Just as the AMS seal didn't eliminate vacuous weather shows, happy news couldn't kill off the serious approach to weather. During the middle and late 1970s, the eastern United States experienced some of its most destructive weather in decades. A record-breaking swarm of tornadoes swept the South and Midwest in 1974; three years later, furious back-to-back winters tore

By the early 1980s, weather sets had become more sophisticated. Bob Ryan and Tom Kierein, at Washington's WRC, had satellite photos and computerized maps at their disposal. (Courtesy WRC)

into the eastern United States with unprecedented cold and snow. Hurricanes David, Frederic, and Allen struck the United States in 1979 and 1980, along with a heat wave in the latter year that caused some 1,000 deaths.

Perhaps in response to these worsening conditions, thoughtful weather coverage made headway in a number of cities. Fresh out of graduate school, Dave Murray went to St. Louis in 1976 to become that area's first television meteorologist. His comprehensive treatment of severe weather helped KSDK vault to the top of local news ratings.[33] On the national level, all three network morning news shows acquired their first true weathercasters between 1977 and 1980. (Murray joined ABC's "Good Morning America" in 1984.)

The growing sophistication of television weather graphics in the late 1970s and early 1980s helped Murray and his serious-weather colleagues display their knowledge on the air. Even media observers were beginning to notice a change as they in turn began to cover television weather with more respect. In a 1980 essay for *Time,* Lance Morrow caught the essence of what seems to bring people to their television sets each night for the weather report.

Are weathercasts necessary? Not absolutely. But ... it is both a comfort
and a convenience to see the national weather satellite pictures, to watch the
migrant storms and bright patches marbling the land, and know just what
kind of weather friends and family are under.[34]

As the 1980s came to a close, television weather was more established
than ever before. A big-city resident with cable television could partake of
dozens of local weathercasts each day (not to mention 24-hour coverage on
The Weather Channel). This viewer might come across a bona fide Ph.D.
expounding on vorticity advection—or a glib announcer who had taken a
single course on weather. "Local color" might be courtesy of a prankster
with a penchant for costumes, or it could be provided by the latest
computer-graphics imagery. Such was the range of television weathercasting as it embarked on its second 50 years.

2

Weathercasting Today

Estimates are that the average American sees over 100,000 television commercials before reaching adulthood. If such figures were tabulated for weathercast viewership, they might also reach well into the thousands. Of course, nobody would watch television for long if every commercial — or every weathercast — were identical. Variety must be present to hold viewer interest. Some of that variety is built into weathercasting through ever-present shifts in the weather.

Yet it's variation within a rigid format that makes for the most durable television programming. Situation comedies and detective shows don't try to remake their genres with each episode. Similarly, weathercasters and their programs share a number of common features, whether they appear in Dubuque or Denver. Nearly every television viewer can recite the standard elements of a weather segment: current conditions, the national map, tomorrow's forecast, and so on.

Beyond the content of a weathercast, a myriad other consistencies shape the world of television weather. Certain kinds of people, with specific backgrounds, appear at given times of day. Even as weathercasters move from station to station and vary their gimmicks, some things about weathercasting almost never change.

WHERE AND WHEN

Just over 1,000 commercial television stations dotted the United States in 1988, with about half broadcasting in the VHF frequency range (channels 2 through 13) and half in UHF (channels 14–69).[1] Nearly all the VHF stations were affiliated with one of three major networks: the National Broadcasting Company (NBC), the American Broadcasting Company (ABC),

15

and the Columbia Broadcasting System (CBS). Most of these stations produce regular local newscasts. Other VHF and UHF stations assemble their
program lineups independent of the networks, and some mount newscasts
rivaling those of their network-affiliated competitors.

Whatever the source, these regular news programs are the heart and
soul of weathercasting, the chance for each weather anchor to hone his or
her skills and develop a rapport with viewers. A remarkable consistency in
stations' scheduling of news has helped some weathercasters amass 20, 30,
or even 40 years of service. Since the 1950s, news broadcasts have been con-
centrated in several distinct periods of the viewing day:

- *Early morning* (6:00–9:00 AM). Many network affiliates begin their
  broadcast day with an hour or half hour of local news, followed
  at or near 7:00 AM (local time) by a network news- entertainment
  mix such as NBC's "Today" or ABC's "Good Morning America."
  Early local newscasts give weather anchors up to 10 minutes of air
  time, broken into several short segments to accommodate viewers
  tuning in midway through the show. Also, network morning
  shows traditionally break at 7:25 and 8:25 AM for a five-minute
  local update. Typically, weather anchors open and close these
  mini-newscasts with perhaps a minute of commuting weather and
  a forecast. Smaller stations commonly forgo a morning weathercaster, letting regular news anchors handle the job.
- *Noon* (12:00–1:00 PM). Firmly in the middle of most people's
  workday, noontime is the least reliable hour for local television
  news. In many large cities, one or two stations will carry a half
  hour of local news while the rest "counterprogram" with daytime
  dramas or talk shows. Small shifts in ratings can spell the quick
  end of a noon newscast and the start of one elsewhere.

  Despite such variability, midday news — when it exists — is a fine
  forum for weathercasters. Sports reports are usually absent from
  a noon show, leaving time for more weather detail than in evening
  newscasts. Agricultural news is a big draw in the nation's heartland, and weather is an integral part of such coverage. Noon
  shows are also a good time to note any potential for severe after-
  noon-and-evening thunderstorms.
- *Early evening* (5:00–7:00 PM). From its humble 15-minute beginnings, the local dinnertime newscast has become a leading profit
  maker for television stations. "Early news," as it's often called,
  can attract audiences as large as that of any other local program.
  Weather plays a consistent, major role in early-evening news.

  A scheduling technique common in the late 1970s and 1980s was
  to sandwich network evening news between two local newscasts,

each an hour or half hour long. This yields as much as 90 minutes for locally originated newscasts, of which 10 to 15 minutes normally goes to weather reports. Smaller stations may limit themselves to a single 30-minute program with perhaps a two- to four-minute weather segment.

The position of weather within a local newscast varies from city to city and station to station. Markets with a high weather consciousness (such as midwestern cities) will usually feature weather between news and sports segments. In larger, less weather-concerned locales, the weather is often shunted to the end of each newscast. However, almost any station will lead its news with a weathercaster if serious storms or other inclement conditions threaten. One news producer in Washington wrote: "Deciding when to lead with a weather-related story is frequently tough.... No matter how well you plan, there will be surprise weather events that will have you scrambling frantically to catch up."[2]

- *News breaks* (7:00–11:00 PM). Following the example set by network news in the 1970s, many if not most affiliate stations now offer one- or two-minute news updates several times nightly during the prime-time viewing hours of 7:00–11:00 PM (7:00–10:00 in the Central and Mountain time zones). While most such briefs feature only a news anchor, some include a 15- or 30-second weather update. Dave Murray (WBZ, Boston) was among the weathercasters doing such regular updates in 1989.

- *Late evening* (10:00 or 11:00 PM, depending on time zone). The viewing public's last look at weather details for the day typically comes with the late-evening news, scheduled at 11:00 PM on the East and West Coasts and 10:00 PM in the nation's midsection. On virtually every United States station, late news runs 30 minutes, with a two- to four-minute weathercast. A number of stations replay their late newscasts after midnight for swing-shift workers and other late-night viewers.

   Some weathercasters find the early evening more conducive to in-depth meteorological discussions and the late evening best for a simpler approach. "At eleven at night, your viewers are half asleep," Frank Field of New York's WCBS told *TV Guide*. "You make your reports as painless as possible. But earlier in the evening, you can be more complete and more technical."[3]

- *Weekends.* Noon shows are absent on Saturday and Sunday; early- and late-evening newscasts tend to be 30 minutes each, with corresponding standard-length weathercasts. Sports events often preempt the early-evening news on Saturdays and Sundays.

WHO AND WHY

Weathercasters in the largest 50–100 markets across the United States share a common order of status within each station. The most coveted, highly paying positions are in weekday evening news shows, while weekday morning and weekend spots are usually taken by either newer, less experienced people or veterans seeking an easier schedule. On the average, each station employs one weathercaster for weekday mornings, another for evenings, and a third for weekends. This formula can vary greatly, though, depending on a station's commitment to news and the weather coverage expected in a particular market. New York's WABC employed only two weathercasters in 1989; one (Storm Field) doubled as a medical-science reporter. In contrast, Tampa's WTVT had five weathercasters—all degreed meteorologists—and a sixth meteorologist to provide off-camera support.

Occasionally, weather is deemphasized to the point of occupying only a minute or two. If big news stories break, weather is often one of the first segments truncated to gain needed time. However, stations that toy with the standard weathercasting format do so at their own risk. Two cases in which weathercasts were completely eliminated show the peril of tampering with television tradition.

New York City's Carol Reed, the first woman to report weather in a large city, became a local legend on WCBS during the 1950s and early 1960s (see Chapter 6). In 1964, her segment was unceremoniously dropped in favor of having regular news anchors read the weather. "We simply intend to put the weather in proper perspective and treat it like any other news," said the WCBS station manager at the time of Reed's dismissal. The decision proved unsuccessful; after 18 months, WCBS resumed standard weathercasts, sans Reed.[4]

St. Louis was no more receptive to newscasts without weathercasting. *TV Guide* noted in early 1977 that the Queen City's KMOX had reduced its standard weather coverage to 30 seconds or less, delivered by the regular news anchor.

> In St. Louis, nobody seems to have missed the weatherman. "We haven't received one piece of mail," says news director Fred Burrows. "The only thing we don't have is a lot of chitchat getting in and out of the weather segment."[5]

Despite the sunny prognosis from *TV Guide,* all was not well with St. Louis' weatherless newscast. "I don't think it lasted any longer than six months," recalls Dave Murray, who did weather on rival station KSDK at the time. "KMOX was a CBS-owned and operated station, so a lot of their directives came right out of New York....They had research that said weather was not very important, and in New York and L.A. that may be true, but I don't think it's to the point where you can eliminate it [from the newscast]."[6]

TRAINING FOR TELEVISION

People arrive at the hybrid vocation of weathercasting from many paths. The sheer variety of weathercasters' backgrounds adds vitality to the profession, insuring that segments across the country will never be totally alike in approach, even as consultants and computers foster a tendency toward standardization.

One of the two main routes to a weathercasting career is a university education in meteorology. Around half of all weathercasters in the largest 50 markets hold bachelor's degrees in meteorology or a closely related physical science. Several dozen schools offer such training; among the most established centers for meteorology education are Pennsylvania State University, the University of Oklahoma, the University of California — Los Angeles, Texas A&M University, and the University of Wisconsin. Most of these meteorology departments sprang up during the field's rapid expansion after World War II.

Students taking physical science and planning a television career can enhance their readiness for weathercasting with courses in speech and/or journalism. (Some students choose to shift the emphasis by majoring in liberal arts and earning a minor in meteorology.) A few schools with strong radio-television departments provide opportunity for hands-on weathercasting in college-produced cable news programs. For example, at least six weathercasters debuting on Oklahoma television in the 1980s appeared on the University of Oklahoma's cable news program while earning meteorology degrees. Such work often ends with videotaping of one or two weathercasts to serve as an electronic resume for television job prospects.

Going a step further, two institutions have devised entire academic programs specifically for weathercasters. Lyndon State College in Lyndonville, Vermont, is a small school with a meteorology department strongly oriented toward weathercasting. Lyndon State offers regular courses on television-weather presentations, along with brief, intensive seminars for non-students.

Another major academic program in weathercasting was founded in 1986 at Mississippi State University (MSU). Much as Lyndon State opens its courses to professionals through seminars, Mississippi State offers up to 30 semester hours through correspondence. The latter option is aimed at practicing weathercasters who want a more complete science background. Hands-on training at both Lyndon State and MSU acquaints students with the computer-graphics equipment now commonly used in television weather.

Some professional scientists make the leap to weathercasting directly from non-television careers in government or industry. The transition can be difficult, though; public-speaking skills are crucial, and mass-market television requires a vocabulary much different from that of scientific interaction. Neil Frank, holder of a Ph.D. in meteorology and director of the National Hurricane Center for 15 years, entered television weather especially late in the game. Frank joined Houston's KHOU in 1988 at the age of 55, after taking early federal retirement. "It was a very, very difficult decision," says Frank, but "it has been a very rewarding experience to relate to people and get them to understand what weather is all about."[7]

A CHOICE OF CREDENTIALS

Training is all well and good, but it's not an absolute requirement for weathercasting. No formal prerequisite exists for every hopeful weather anchor. That openness has brought about a great diversity of weathercasters; it has also produced consternation in those who would prefer a higher standard. Two voluntary certification programs now exist for weathercasters who want to put a symbol of authority behind their work.

The American Meteorological Society's seal of approval for radio or television weathercasting is the older, more esteemed, and more popular of the seal-granting programs. It was created out of concern over gimmicky weathercasts during the mid-1950s (see Chapter 1). Only 65 people received AMS seals in the program's first decade, 1959–1968. One reason for the seal's slow growth was its stipulation that recipients must be eligible for full membership status in the AMS. In essence, that required a bachelor's degree in atmospheric science or five years of work as a meteorologist. While this restriction made the seal a rare and valued honor, it also ruled out awarding seals to those people who strove for accurate, detailed weathercasts but had no degrees.

Noting "the expansion of news broadcasts and environmental awareness," AMS leaders voted in October 1972 to allow seal applications from nonmeteorologists with at least three years of weathercasting experience. To compensate for their lack of training in meteorology, these people had to pass a written examination.[8]

At first, the more inclusive seal did not skyrocket in popularity. Only about 10 to 15 people received seals each year in the mid-1970s. The AMS rescinded its 1972 seal changes somewhat in 1977, now specifying five years of television experience for nonmeteorologist applicants instead of three.[9] It was after that revision, ironically, that AMS seal awards became far

Recipients of the American Meteorological Society seal of approval often display their award on the air. Jack Capell, of Portland's KGW, is shown here with a 1960s depiction of the seal. (Courtesy KGW)

more commonplace. Just five seals were granted in 1977, but 33 were awarded in 1978 and 36 in 1979. By September 1981, 236 people held the seal of approval.

While dilution of the seal's distinctiveness may have worried AMS leaders, a more pressing concern seems to have been the threat of lawsuits from disgruntled applicants and others. That fear was apparently the motive for a surprise decision from the AMS in October 1981 that restored the seal's original restriction to professional meteorologists. The rationale behind this move was summarized rather obliquely in the *Bulletin of the American Meteorological Society:*

> It has always been the goal of the Seal of Approval program to foster high standards of professionalism among broadcast meteorologists. Recently, however, the courts have attacked the use of the term "professionalism" as being overbroad and capable of misuse. Indeed, this standard has many different meanings to different individuals.[10]

Whatever the reasoning behind it, the tightening of seal requirements was a major setback to many nondegreed weathercasters who had hoped to earn seals. In February 1982, only four months later, an alternate credential for weathercasters was founded by the National Weather Association (NWA). The NWA had begun in 1976 as a smaller, more informal alternative to the AMS. In keeping with that philosophy, the NWA Certification of Television (or Radio) Weathercasting required no degree and no written test. Other facts of the program were much like those of the AMS seal: Applicants sent a videotape of one of their weather segments to an NWA committee, which ranked the broadcast in five categories. Successful applicants could display the NWA logo on their weathercasts.[11] As might be expected from its more lenient requirements, the NWA certification program grew quickly. By late 1984, 86 television and radio weathercasters had earned NWA recognition.[12]

SCIENCE AND SHOW BIZ

Since television weather is a blend of scientific exposition and entertainment, some people enter the field after successful careers in the latter. Such was the case for legions of 1950s weathercasters who had ample presence and speaking skill but little knowledge of the atmosphere. For some, a brief period of doing television weather is only a prelude to greater ambitions. Others develop a liking for the weathercast routine and decide to stick with it, picking up formal or informal meteorological training as they see fit.

Willard Scott, one of America's best-known weathermen, became a celebrity on Washington's radio and television almost two decades before doing weather. His WRC career began in 1950 when he served as a page for WRC radio. Scott later gained local fame as a member of radio's "Joy Boys" comedy team and as television's Bozo the Clown. When a WRC weathercaster abruptly left in 1967, Scott filled in. The temporary assignment lasted 13 years, even though Scott had no background in meteorology.[13]

In a similar fashion, Sam Shad came to the United States from England planning a career in radio, only to gravitate to weathercasting. Shad was a disc jockey at a Reno, Nevada, nightclub in 1979 when he began doing weekend weather at Reno's KOLO. He stayed in Reno and in television weather through the 1980s, moving to rival KTVN in 1985. "I don't pretend to be a meteorologist, but I feel it is important for the viewers to get the most accurate information available," Shad told the *American Weather Observer*.[14]

For people like Scott and Shad, a meteorology degree isn't essential to providing the public with the weather information it needs. That view is largely justified: A complete weathercast can be put together simply by acquiring the mountains of data available through the National Weather

Service or private meteorological firms. However, the nonmeteorologist is at a distinct disadvantage when weather changes occur quickly and last-minute developments aren't covered by the Weather Service. A weather-caster who has well-grounded knowledge in meteorology, if not a degree, can adapt Weather Service information to reflect the very latest conditions.

Like many nonmeteorologists doing television weather, Shad is eager to learn more and quick to acknowledge help from the government. "I make use of the expert information from the National Weather Service here in Reno to convey the weather to the viewing public. And I take an active interest in learning and sharing more information about weather and climate."[15]

A CLOSER LOOK AT WEATHERCASTING

What finally emerges from all the above scheduling and training? How does the average day of a weathercaster unfold? These questions can best be answered by visiting two weathermen as they go about their duties in two very different cities: Bob Ryan, at WRC in Washington, D.C. (the nation's ninth largest television market out of the top 212 in 1988) and Harry Spohn, at KNOP in North Platte, Nebraska (the third smallest market among the 212).[16]

Bob Ryan, WRC

The studios of WRC television are nestled in a parklike setting of northwest Washington, several miles from the United States Capitol complex.[17] WRC has a long and colorful weathercasting history, beginning with Louis Allen in 1948 (when the station's call letters were WNBW). Willard Scott became a Washington favorite doing weather from 1967 until 1980 when he was tapped for NBC's "Today." As Scott joined that program, Bob Ryan traded places with him, moving from "Today" to WRC. Ryan has since completed nearly a decade at WRC, building a large weather staff and a program known for its technical wizardry.

On this late-winter Monday afternoon, a brooding deck of stratus clouds hangs over Washington. Ryan occasionally glances at the thickening cloud bank from his second-floor office window as he quickly but calmly prepares graphics for his 5:00 PM weathercast. At 3:45, he has little more than an hour to create the array of electronic maps that make his weather-casts distinctive.

Surrounding Ryan is a cornucopia of electronics, photos, and weather data. One wall is covered with press clippings, National Weather Service releases, letters from viewers, and other paraphernalia. Across from this is

Much of the preparation time for Bob Ryan's weathercast is spent at a computer terminal. Ryan moves frontal systems on a television monitor (right) using a stylus and tablet (center).

a photo of the Earth, taken from the Moon, that fills an entire wall. Below Earth is a long, low desk bearing several CRT screens and computer keyboards. This is the locus of Ryan's job, the workstation at which he creates and assembles ten-second pieces of weather graphic video.

At the heart of Ryan's graphics system is a "Liveline IV," one of the immensely popular series of packages designed specifically for television weather by ColorGraphics Systems, Inc. The Liveline comes with a vast supply of geographic backgrounds, weather symbols, map projections, and the like, all of which can be arranged as the weathercaster likes. Today, Ryan wants to show the fitful progress of a front over the Southeast. He agrees with the National Weather Service that a wave of low pressure scooting along the front will give D.C. a shot of snow, although he expects nothing major.

With several flicks of a stylus across the Liveline's instrument pad, Ryan moves a red L (symbolizing the wave) along a computer-depicted front on the television monitor. Each movement of the low and the front is keyed into the system individually, so that the entire sequence — spanning over 24 hours of weather — can be replayed in a few seconds. Once ready, Ryan loads the loop, and the low slides from Tennessee into the Atlantic Ocean, just as planned. Such computer artistry became standard in television weather during the 1980s.

"The technology is interesting," Ryan says. "With satellite delivery of modern information systems, it's possible for even a station in Grand Island, Nebraska, to dial up and get a color-enhanced satellite and also have radar at their disposal. Twenty years ago, there were a bunch of limitations."

As for radar, something Ryan might use on tonight's 10:00 PM show, WRC chooses to tap the National Weather Service radar at Patuxent River, Maryland, rather than installing its own. "We're waiting for NEXRAD to come on line [the Next Generation Weather Radar network, planned for the 1990s by the National Weather Service and other federal agencies]. By using Pax River radar, it gets us out of the ground clutter of Washington.* There are other stations that have had some problems [with ground clutter], especially when you're right in the middle of Washington."

At 4:00 PM, Ryan dashes to the next room, which doubles as overflow workspace for his office and a television studio for quick weather updates. Against the partition dividing the two rooms is a large green-felt map of the Washington metropolitan area, with a set of stick-on numbers for indicating temperatures. A single television camera is wedged into the far corner, which opens into a mini-newsroom analogous to Ryan's mini-studio for weather. (The full-scale news set is downstairs.)

After a few seconds of headlines from the news anchor, Ryan breezes into an instant summation of the sloppy weather expected that night. Less than a minute later, he's back at his workstation. Ryan and his fellow weathercasters at WRC appear on these hourly updates between 7:00 AM and 4:00 PM each weekday.

Through the critical 4:00–5:00 PM period, Ryan methodically pieces his weather segment together. Phone calls to Ryan from station personnel are kept short, almost telegraphic: "The last frame's got a glitch in it." "Hi there ... OK ..." "I'm not sure, I think A-1 ... Sure." Underneath the calls is the constant chatter of a high-speed printer spewing out weather data; filtering into Ryan's office is the hurried conversation of newsroom employees rushing to make deadlines. Yet Ryan seems utterly unfazed by the crescendo of activity around him. Having already examined the National Weather Service forecast maps hanging on the wall to his right, he focuses on putting the weather scenario from his mind into the computer. Only briefly does he glance at the Weather Service data.

Experience helps Ryan navigate the preshow frenzy. He came to weather from the university pipeline, earning a bachelor's degree in physics and an M.S. in meteorology from the State University of New York, Albany. Interested in cloud physics, Ryan then landed work with a private consulting firm in Boston, designing research instruments.

Ground clutter is the term for radar echoes produced by structures near the radar antenna, rather than by precipitation.

"I always had it in the back of my mind that it'd be fun to try TV. I talked to Don Kent (WBZ, Boston), who was sort of the dean of New England weathercasters, and he encouraged me to go on."

Ryan's first television stint, a late-night position at a Boston UHF station, enabled him to continue full-time research work. The station's newscast ended nine months after Ryan's arrival, "but by that time, I'd gotten a little bit of the bug." Next came a morning weather job in Providence, Rhode Island, which forced Ryan to go part-time at his research job. He joined Boston's WCVB full-time in 1972, leaving research for good, and went to NBC's "Today" in 1978.

The pace in WRC's newsroom actually slows as 5:00 PM approaches; most of the crucial work is done, and news anchors are heading downstairs to the main set. Ryan stays at his desk, hardly blinking at the top of the hour, making last-minute changes to a new map he'll incorporate tonight. It depicts the next day's weather in animation from a satellite's vantage point, with the moon and sun passing over the earth's contour as fronts move west to east. Ryan's goal is to segue from a satellite loop of the day's weather (furnished by Environmental Satellite Data, Inc.) into the next day's forecast without changing perspective. "Rather than just snapping between two different projections, it kind of eases your eye," he says.

From the other half of Ryan's office, an amplified answering machine picks up phone calls from WRC "weather watchers," the loose-knit network of viewers scattered through the D.C. area who report weather from their homes: ". . . a cool overnight low of twenty-seven, and at five o'clock it is thirty-four degrees, and we've had cloudy skies all day," reports one viewer. "Have yourself a nice evening." This and other observations will be plotted by an assistant for use on the weathercast.

Finally, at 5:10, Ryan sprints out of his office and through a maze of corridors and stairwells to the first-floor studio. It's a surprisingly small room, perhaps 50 by 50 feet in area, with the news set angled in one corner, two weather maps along the opposite wall, and cameras clustered in the middle. After a commercial break, during which Ryan clips on a microphone and sits next to the news anchors, the show is on.

Old and new weathercast styles mingle on Ryan's program. His opening chat with the news anchors is a 30-second ritual nonexistent in television weather before 1970 but now standard procedure. One anchor asks Ryan, "So what's going on? What's this talk of snow?" He responds, "Some wet snowflakes. You know, we had some over the weekend. Did you see it?" "I did. It wasn't enough," replies the anchor, a winter-weather fan, laughing.

After a little more introduction, Ryan then strolls to his dual weather maps. To the right is a solid-green chromakey screen, the backdrop against which computer images are placed in the outgoing television signal. Ryan does the first two-thirds of his program with chromakey, gesturing at the empty board while watching his movements on a television monitor discreetly placed above both maps. (Though available since the 1950s, chromakey didn't greatly affect television weather until the early 1980s.)

The segment begins with a look at the lengthening days of late February as Ryan shows a special graphic. Then comes the national map: "There's a weather front that separates some rather warm, moist air to our south from cooler air to our north. Along that front, a series of little, weak low-pressure areas will scurry by. One will move out tonight. . . . Take away the clouds," he says, having jumped to the satellite picture and then to a radar depiction, "and you can see where the precipitation is right now. . . ."

The last part of Ryan's segment takes place before the second wall fixture, a nonelectronic depiction of the entire Chesapeake Bay region. Affixed to the map are six-inch numbers representing temperatures reported by the WRC weather watchers. Before this somewhat old-fashioned graphic, Ryan gives his outlook and (in the oldest weathercasting tradition of all) uses removable paint to highlight the regions where snow will be heaviest. "Some of the grassy areas will whiten up, but the streets should see temperatures above freezing," he says. "To the south, you folks may see a little bit more snow, maybe an inch or two down around the Fredericksburg area, but there it will also likely mix with some rain and be kind of a sloppy mess.

"A little touch of winter, but nothing bad," Ryan says in summation, returning to the news anchors' desk after his 3½-minute segment. The anchors go on to another commercial break as Ryan leaves the studio for his office and more work on the 6:00 PM show.

The blend of old and new in Ryan's weathercast is a deliberate choice. "I still like having the [nonelectronic] local maps. That way, like I did today, I can go over and draw in things. It gives a touch that you can't get with chromakey. Plus, you become a conduit for the information."

Harry Spohn, KNOP

For a contrast to the big-city hubbub of Washington, D.C., it would be hard to do better than North Platte, Nebraska.[18] The city of 25,000 is cradled at the intersection of the North Platte and South Platte rivers, which merge in the west-central part of the state. Aside from a few large river towns, western Nebraska is virtually unpopulated. Counties bigger than Delaware or Rhode Island have only a few thousand farmers and ranchers.

The studios of KNOP, North Platte's only television station, are perched on a hill several miles north of town. Although the KNOP building is weatherbeaten, and the facilities are hardly brand-new, there is an air of pride among the staff. KNOP recently won "Best Newscast in Nebraska" honors from the state Associated Press, beating out much larger rivals in Lincoln and Omaha.

On this warm June evening, Harry Spohn is decked out in a blazer, rodeo-style belt, and cowboy boots. The weathercaster is saluting Nebraskaland Days, an annual celebration during which state residents are urged to wear Western attire. As is common in small-city television, Spohn welcomes the chance to be civic booster for a night.

Preparation for Spohn's late-evening show begins around 8:00 PM when he grabs a sheaf of teletyped weather data and heads to his desk. Spoh's "office" is actually a corner of the news set, with a single partition carving out perhaps 100 square feet of work area. Against the partition is the makeup mirror shared by news and sports anchors. File cabinets and an aging wooden desk make up the other side of Spohn's territory.

Though he lacks the elbowroom of Bob Ryan and other big-city weathercasters, Spohn doesn't seem hindered by the circumstances. Between now and 10:00 PM, he'll be dashing around the KNOP building, spending as much time outside as inside his office.

Getting to work, Spohn takes a red felt-tip pen and starts placing forecast temperatures for the next day (Saturday) from the teletyped copy onto a glass-surfaced map of Nebraska. A weak front pushed through North Platte earlier in the day, triggering heavy thunderstorms to the southeast. Spohn drapes the front across Nebraska with a blue marker, estimating its position from current observations. "Cooler than 80's" is the heading Spohn puts on top of the map, but he's skeptical.

"I don't think it'll be as cold as they're saying, frankly," he confides. "I'll take one more look at Grand Island's temperature before making a decision." After checking, he decides to raise his forecast high from the National Weather Service's cooler prediction.

Spohn's off-the-cuff forecasting is part necessity and part tradition. KNOP lacks the budget for the facsimile maps nearly every station receives, much less the computerized graphics found in most cities' television weather. Spohn must hand-draw his maps from teletype data alone. However, a long career with the National Weather Service gave him the instinct for weather patterns needed for such a task.

Born and raised in the Los Angeles area, Spohn joined the navy just after World War II. He served three years, then went to Chicago for an ill-fated try at accounting school. "I found out six months into the class that I would never be a CPA if I lived to be a hundred. To me, a person who deals with figures has a mental image of their field of work.... I couldn't picture myself doing profit-loss statements." A brief period of career uncertainty followed, ending with the Korean War when Spohn was called to active duty as a weather observer in Japan. That year of immersion in meteorology got Spohn interested in the field and gave him the training needed to land a Weather Bureau spot.

From 1953 through 1984, Spohn served the bureau in a number of locales. The most exotic stint — the one that gave Spohn a glimpse of the television life — was a 13-month stay in Antarctica. On July 13, 1963, Spohn recorded an air temperature of $-109.8°$ F, the lowest ever measured to that date by a Weather Bureau employee. The experience made Spohn enough of a celebrity for an interview on NBC's "Today" in December 1963. More television exposure came during Spohn's ten years as the supervisor of North Platte's National Weather Service office, when he did monthly five-minute education segments on KNOP.

Having done such television work, it was an easy transition for Spohn after retirement from the NWS to become North Platte's first and only weathercaster. The station had been using news anchors to deliver weather: "They never had a full-fledged weatherperson. Somebody would do the news and weather, or maybe they'd do weather and sports. When I approached the management of the station and told them I was going to be available, the answer was yes."

Spohn now revels in the independence of his own weather show after decades in the more fettered world of government. Within an hour's time on this June evening, he has a map of Nebraska marked in the standard Weather Service color scheme for fronts, precipitation, and the like. The front positions are his own best guess, with the teletyped data as a guideline. Spohn takes the map and places them on the wall next to the news anchors' seats; a camera will add it to Spohn's weathercast via chromakey.

At 9:30, Spohn has less than an hour to finalize his segment. The next 20 minutes find him shuttling between:

- the teletype room, for 9:00 PM observations and the latest national summary;
- a video monitor, where a national satellite loop and several computer graphics are regularly sent from WRC in Washington and taped for Spohn's show (the service was created by NBC for its smaller affiliates);
- a character generator, one of the graphic tools found in stations large and small. Here, Spohn oversees a production assistant entering statistics and "Harry's Forecast." These will be displayed at the beginning and end of Spohn's weathercast, filling the screen with text over a brightly colored background while Spohn adds commentary.

One more stop for Spohn this evening is an audio control booth, where he records a brief update to be broadcast on North Platte radio the next

Both national and state maps are complete as Harry Spohn places them for use on his weather-cast.

morning. Finally, with 10:00 PM approaching, he returns to his desk. National-weather summary in hand, he sketches fronts and temperatures on a second glass-covered map. In ten minutes (less time than it might take to generate a similar map with computers), Spohn takes the finished product and hangs it over the Nebraska map to be chromakeyed.

News anchors fill the studio and young cameramen engage in Friday-night joking as Spohn dons his jacket and dabs on makeup. Unlike the WRC early newscast, KNOP opens this late show with a shot of all the on-camera talent, Spohn included. In the ten minutes between that opening and his segment, Spohn checks last-minute teletype reports. He finds that a tornado warning has just been issued for one Nebraska county near Lincoln. However, the state's capital city is 250 miles east of North Platte, well outside KNOP's viewing area.

Such a storm to the north or west might have caused Spohn more concern. An extra transmitter near the town of Thedford gives KNOP a much greater range in those directions where media outlets are practically nonexistent and KNOP's importance is thus magnified. Some homes in north-central Nebraska receive only a single television station (KNOP), and one 50,000-watt radio signal. Spohn's years at the North Platte NWS office involved regular visits to such isolated locales, making him especially conscious of their needs. He often goes beyond his two-shows-a-day, six-days-a-week schedule to give bulletins during severe weather.

During this program's second commercial break, Spohn strolls to the news set and takes a seat. The KNOP anchors open his segment with the obligatory small talk; Spohn banters back. Then, while he strolls across the studio to his chromakey backdrop, an NBC satellite picture fills the screen, accompanied by Spohn's low-key but brisk description of the day's thunderstorm activity. "Right now, all the action's over in the Omaha-Lincoln area. They've had hail at Buckley, and they also had a tornado touch down near Crete, Nebraska, which is about twenty miles south of Lincoln. . . ."

In keeping with North Platte's location in the nation's heartland, Spohn devotes the first half of his show to national weather, accompanied by one of his hand-drawn maps. "Out to the west, there's nothing but warm air. A hundred and four at Palm Springs, California — of course, that's in the desert. Gunnison, Colorado, was the nation's low this morning at twenty-eight."

Concluding the national discussion is a computer-generated forecast map from WRC. Spohn then shifts viewer attention to Nebraska with a set of text graphics giving North Platte conditions and statistics. A state summary, with Spohn's second hand-drawn map, follows. Wrapping up the weathercast are the state and local forecasts ("For the daytime Saturday, variable cloudiness. Maybe you'll see the sun a little bit, but look for some showers in the afternoon").

Spohn considers his three- to four-minute forum an extension of his work in the National Weather Service. The most satisfying part of that career for Spohn was providing severe weather warnings: "I was in the government for thirty-one years. In that entire period, I had exactly two people thank me for saving their life in a tornado situation. What greater thing can one person do for another human being?" As for television weather, says Spohn, "It's just a continuation of being of service."

On July 25, 1989, only a few days after this interview, Harry Spohn found himself "being of service" to North Platte in a very big way. A tornado cut across the north edge of town, damaging over a dozen homes. But thanks to a prompt warning issued by the North Platte NWS and broadcast by Spohn, no serious injuries occurred.

Just before eight that evening a viewer called Spohn to report a funnel

Spohn joins his KNOP colleagues as the newscast wraps up.

cloud. He referred her to the NWS, which acted quickly. "We went on the air at eight o'clock with the official tornado warning," says Spohn. Shortly thereafter, as reports of downed trees and power lines came in, Spohn realized that KNOP might be forced off the air. "We went on the air again at twelve minutes past the hour, updating for the tornado and advising counties upstream that the storm was heading their way." Four minutes later, KNOP lost all power. Unable to broadcast, Spohn and colleagues went outside and watched the tornado pass within a quarter mile of KNOP, tearing across a subdivision. His early warnings made the difference to residents of that area: "Our newspaper [the North Platte *Telegraph*] printed a tornado special in which one of the families from Hillcrest Estates gave me credit for saving their lives."[19]

3

From Silly to Serious

If science has a defining stereotype in the public eye, it's that of the cold, unfeeling, analytical scientist, interested only in his lab results, unable to communicate with others except in desiccated jargon. That long-standing myth, though less prevalent in recent years, continues to resonate in pop culture. As late as 1982, the movie *E.T.* portrayed government scientists as the unalloyed villains.

Ironically, the biggest showcase for science that television has had since its founding — the daily weather report — could hardly be more distant from that stereotype. Some weathercasters do favor a sober, technical approach, but humor and energy are far more common attributes of the weathercast. Costumes, chickens, cartoons, and children have all paraded through weathercasts, making the news anchor, if anyone, seem staid.

In television as in no other medium, style consistently dominates substance. People may rely on the information from weathercasts to help them plan their day, but what sticks in the public memory year in and year out is less a particular forecast than a weathercaster's persona, his or her gimmicks, patter, and philosophy. While gimmicky weathercasts may be a disservice to the serious practice of meteorology, they do strike an undeniable blow at the homogenized, prepackaged nature of most television of the 1980s. Those who long for the spontaneity that left prime-time television with the advent of film and videotape can take heart: That spirit lives on each day in the live, ad-libbed world of television weather.

CREATING THE STYLE

Radio weather preceded television by some 20 years, but it hardly set a precedent for the wild variety of television weathercasts. From the 1920s through the 1940s, weather was news — no more and usually no less. Most stations assigned weather to their regular news anchors, and the forecast was delivered in their usual serious, straightforward fashion.

The few weather specialists on radio in those days adhered to the going standard for news delivery. These men, usually meteorologists, were the forerunners of what might be called the just-the-facts school of weathercasting. The emphasis was on the atmosphere alone; little embellishment was provided beyond comments on the more unusual weather happenings of the day.

James Fidler billed himself as Radio's Original Weatherman in 1938 while broadcasting on WBLC in Muncie, Indiana. His down-to-earth description of national weather is a prime example of just-the-facts reporting:

> "That is the picture of the weather map. Now, we will look at the Weather Bureau statistics for the past twenty-four hours for some unusual reports and possibly some new records. First, the highest temperature reported in the country for the past twenty-four hours was at Fresno, California, where the Weather Bureau reports a maximum of seventy-eight degrees."[1]

Fidler stressed dependability. Upon entering television in 1948, he stressed that weathercasters "should always appear sincere and confident."[2] Thorough and accurate if unembellished, Fidler's style was echoed by many early weathercasters.

Stronger influences were on the way, though. Television carried its own set of demands, specific and quite different from radio's. Francis Davis, a Philadelphia radio meteorologist, told the American Meteorological Society of his first television-weather experience in 1948: "Television has been tried but abandoned: the weather from Washington covered too much territory, and the presentation was too static."[3]

Davis' comment is a telling one. Actual weather is in constant flux, but nothing is more static than a single weather map. Until technology could make the maps move (a step that took decades), weathercasters themselves had to provide the action, both in vivid language and in animated movement.

In that sense, the earliest prototype of the modern television weatherman was Louis Allen. Allen was a scientist with bachelor's and master's degrees in meteorology who combined weather knowledge with a flair for the accessible. One technique Allen used was the personification of weather-map features such as temperature contours:

> "And here's our old friend the seventy-five-degree line.... At the moment, no sign anywhere near us of that old bugaboo the ninety-degree line that

kept us stewing for awhile. But looks as if we might have more warm weather before fall sets in."[4]

As "unscientific" as it may be to endow an abstract concept with human qualities, the technique does bring dry data to life. Allen's anthropomorphic fronts and temperature lines became television-weather standbys to the point of becoming clichés.

Another invention of Allen's that paved the way for other weathercasters was his daily "doodle." At the end of each five-minute show, Allen preceded the official forecast by drawing a quick sketch that symbolized the next day's expected weather. For example, a picture of two boys on swings denoted warm weather appropriate for outdoor play. (The doodle concept grew out of drawings sent to Allen by his wife during World War II, when Allen was a military forecaster.)[5]

Using cartoons to illustrate the weather wasn't totally unprecedented; experimental stations in the early 1940s had done just that. What made Allen's doodles groundbreaking was their off-the-cuff creation. Instead of spending time before the show drawing an exceptional picture, Allen chose to maximize television's appetite for motion by sketching while on camera. The result was a less detailed drawing but a far more involving technique. Less than a year after Allen began, he had a waiting list of children to be given each day's doodle.[6] Other weathercasters noticed Allen's doodling or came up with the notion themselves as an onslaught of cartoon characters invaded weathercasts over the next few years.

With Louis Allen's informal yet informative weather reporting came the realization that television could present weather in a lighthearted fashion. From that idea sprang the enormous variety of gimmicks that came to characterize television weather. Yet compared to some of the more flamboyant weathercasters that followed him, Allen's technique seems almost sedate. With Jimmie Fidler's very down-to-earth approach at one pole and Willard Scott's hijinks at the other, Louis Allen falls very much in between — as good an example of the "average" weathercaster as any.

PUPPETS AND PICTURES

"Kukla, Fran and Ollie" was one of television's first hit shows, a children's series featuring two lively puppets and a low-key host. The marionette Howdy Doody was another early smash. Television weatherpeople took a cue from these hits in the 1950s, as cartoon characters and puppets appeared by the dozens on local television-weather shows. Such creations added distinctiveness to weathercasts and allowed for interaction on what was otherwise a one-person segment.

The dean of New York City weathercast creations was Uncle Wethbee, a standby of Tex Antoine's WABC segments for over 20 years. Wethbee was affixed to a wall next to the day's forecast. His handlebar mustache was keyed to the outlook, drooping or curling based on the expected conditions. Wethbee's clothing also gave weather clues; the puppet would appear with a wig in brisk weather or a stocking cap for bitter cold. Antoine once described Uncle Wethbee as a way to put "sugar coating on a rather dull subject."[7]

In many other cities, puppets were similarly used to hint at the upcoming forecast. A close runner-up to Uncle Wethbee in sheer longevity was Albert the Alleycat, who accompanied weather on Milwaukee's WITI from the 1950s through 1972.[8] At Chicago's WBBM, P. J. Hoff employed a set of two-dimensional paper creations representing different weather forces; the puppets battled it out on a weather map under Hoff's direction. For example, Susanna South Wind would be shown moving toward Nanook North Wind if a warm-up was expected.[9] Wind velocities were once reported on a St. Louis station by Windermere (Windy) P. Redundant.[10] Another option for weathercasters was creating puppets tied to a specific city. Senator Fairweather appeared on Washington television in the 1950s.

Weathercasters with a flair for pen and ink followed in Louis Allen's footsteps and devised their own cartoon characters. One classic example is Gusty, a round-headed sprite that appeared for 35 years on Don Woods' weathercasts at KTUL in Tulsa. Woods drew a Gusty portrait each day that illustrated the dominant weather theme. On a windy day, for example, Gusty might be found clinging to a tree. The character's simplicity and versatility made him something of a Tulsa legend. Woods trademarked his creation and received thousands of requests for original Gusty portraits. A rendition of Gusty resides in the Smithsonian Institution's permanent collection of modern American folk art.[11]

One weathercaster continuing the cartoon tradition is Linda Gialanella at Philadelphia's KYW. Gialanella won the 1973 Miss America talent competition for her impromptu sketches and narration. That skill serves her well in the spontaneous format of television weather, where she adds humorous drawings to her forecasts. In 1986, Gialanella received a local Emmy award for artistic direction.

ANIMALS ... AND OTHER CIRCUS ACTS

Should a puppet or drawing not bring enough human interest to the weathercast, there's always been the option of using nonhumans. The range of animals brought to weather segments has been limited only by the imagination of weathercasters (to the dismay of animal-rights advocates). While

With his informative yet casual style, Louis Allen (shown in 1948 at WNBW, Washington, now WRC) set a precedent for television weather nationwide. (Courtesy *Bulletin of the American Meteorological Society*)

the use of animated characters on weathercasts peaked in the 1950s, the idea of trotting out animals seemed to crest during the 1970s' proliferation of happy-news formats. Some examples from that decade:

- George Fischbeck of Los Angeles' KABC brought a lion and a lamb into his studio to commemorate the arrival of March.[12]
- Lloyd Lindsay Young in Evansville, Indiana, delivered one weathercast accompanied by a pig.[13]
- A weathercaster in Savannah, Georgia, reportedly interacted with a seagull during his shows.[14]
- While at Chicago's WLS, John Coleman read his Thanksgiving Day forecast one year to a turkey.[15]

Perhaps the apex of this bizarre trend is animals' replacing the weathercaster. This occurred at KDBC in El Paso during the late 1970s when a dog named Puffy Little Cloud became the regular weather anchor. Puffy (a Lhasa apso) appeared each day in an outfit appropriate to the day's weather, while an off-camera announcer served as the dog's "voice," reading weather details.[16] Not to be outdone, KATU in Portland, Oregon, has featured Bob the Weather Cat weekly since 1983. Like Puffy Little Cloud, Bob wears an outfit suiting the daily conditions, as well as such

One of the longest-running cartoon characters in television weather was Gusty, created and trademarked by Don Woods of Tulsa's KTUL. Woods appeared on KTUL from 1954 to 1989. Shown here is Gusty in good fishing weather. (Courtesy Don Woods, KTUL)

seasonal costumes as a Santa suit. Bumper stickers, fan mail, and a line of greeting cards attest to Bob's popularity in Portland.[17]

Certainly, if puppets and dogs can wear clothes as a shorthand means of giving the weather outlook, humans can too. This technique was popular among "weathergirls" during their 1950s peak in popularity. Janet Tyler of New York City's WABC specialized in hats fitting the expected conditions (or an umbrella to denote rain).[18] But weathercasters soon found costumes to be far more than mere reflections of the forecast. Over more than two decades, Willard Scott has taken the possibilities of creative weathercasting to unrivaled lengths. Scott appeared on Washington's WRC dressed as George Washington, Robin Hood, and a kilted Scot, among other characters. On NBC's "Today," he gave one memorable weathercast as the 1940s singer Carmen Miranda, complete with flowing skirt and feathered headdress. In 1984, Scott followed up as androgynous pop singer Boy George.[19]

In contrast to Scott's variety of outfits, some weathercasters relied on a specific costumed persona. New Orleans residents got television weather in the early 1960s from "Morgus the Magnificent," a refugee from WWL's "House of Shock" horror-movie series. Complete with lab coat, plastic fangs, and a wig, Morgus delivered statistics in an appropriately ghoulish fashion. "Ninety-eight degrees is the temperature at which a frog's eye boils in water," he once reported.[20]

Top banana of the weather clowns is Willard Scott, seen on NBC's "Today" since 1980. One of his earliest "Today" stunts was dressing as singer Carmen Miranda. (Courtesy NBC)

WEATHER WORDS

Language is another means for weathercasters to make their deliveries distinctive. While temperature and wind data wouldn't seem a natural source of vivid phrases, their variations and the constant movement of weather systems give weatherpeople a chance to embroider their program with puns, allusions, double entendres, and other wordplay.

Some weathercasters find ways to announce the most mundane of statistics in an entertaining fashion. Along with the visual gimmick of Uncle Wethbee, Tex Antoine had a distinct verbal hook. The science magazine *Discover* observed in 1985 that Antoine's "almost jazzlike patter had drawn a cult following."

"One-oh-five this afternoon, we hit the high for the day of five-one," he
would say. "We first hit our low, we are matching it now, as I said, at three-
fifty this morning, four-oh. We won't drift off too much, but if June in
January doesn't amaze you, would you take a little April?"[21]

Antoine's manner of speaking was more an idiosyncrasy than a style
emulated by others. Much more common in weathercasting is simple pun-
nery. Bob Weaver, of Miami's WTVJ, the city's longest-running weathercaster, has indulged in puns through more than three decades on the
air. Viewers in High Point, N.C., have heard such phrases as "puddle up
a little closer," "a streetcar named perspire," and "unidentified frying objects."

Lively phrases of a more general nature also embroider some weathercasts. Sonny Eliot became a master of meteorological metaphor in his three
decades on WWJ in Detroit. Eliot's descriptions of weather ranged from
"colder than the seat of the last man on a short toboggan" to "uncomfor-
table as a swordfish with an ingrown nose."[22] Another sample of Eliot's
phrases: "The storm center is still up there, as ominous as a skunk with an
upraised tail. It's continuing to move toward the northeast, but slower than
a nudist climbing a barbed-wire fence."[23]

Eliot also made his mark as a linguist by coining words to describe
weather combinations. These included "fozzle" (fog and drizzle), "crazy"
(crisp and hazy), "pleezy" (pleasantly breezy), and "snowsy" (snowy and
lousy). In the Eliot tradition, Fred Norman, of KOCO in Oklahoma City,
has spoken of "snirt" (snow and dirt or dust). Such compounds actually
have a precedent in serious meteorology. The term *smog* originated as a
description of simultaneous smoke and fog (though it later came to denote
pollution in general).

KEEPING A STRAIGHT FACE:
THE SERIOUS APPROACH

Through decades of gimmickry, a sizable number of weathercasters have
maintained the straightforward delivery of their radio pioneers. Conces-
sions must often be made to the visual medium, such as a weathercast
delivered outdoors or a showy set of graphics. But instead of being the cen-
terpiece of a weathercast, these serve more as adornments to the real focus
of attention — weather itself.

The serious approach to weathercasting got a head start in the late
1940s, before "funny weather" had even been conceived. Radio meteorologists and their sober style were joined by World War II veterans and
Weather Bureau retirees with more background in science than entertain-

ment. *Time* observed in 1968: "In the beginning, weathermen talked so much about 'occluded fronts' and 'thermal inversions' that viewers wondered if they shouldn't start building an ark in the backyard."[24]

Yet by the mid-1950s, lighthearted weather, long on stunts and usually short on information, had taken over. It wasn't until 1959 that the scientific community's distaste for this trend resulted in the American Meteorological Society's seal-of-approval program. With this visible affirmation came a slow increase in respect for the serious approach. That trend slackened in the early 1970s as "happy news" dominated the airwaves, but resumed full force in the late 1970s and 1980s, thanks in part to an explosion in weather-graphic possibilities. The new technology, with its densely informative maps, was an easy way for knowledgeable weathercasters to provide colorful yet accurate data.

Professor Weathercaster

What are the hallmarks of the serious weathercaster? Education ranks at the top, in both training and philosophy. Certainly, possessing a meteorology degree gives a weathercaster more authority than an unschooled competitors. But even more important than the presence or lack of formal credentials is a willingness to respect weather as a field of inquiry and an ability to convey that attitude to the public.

"We like to do a bit of education without making it seem like Meteorology 101," says Bob Ryan of Washington's WRC. (Ryan considered a high school teaching career before going into weathercasting.) "I have a lot of fun with the weather.... I think if you're trained in what you're doing and interested in what you're doing, your enthusiasm will come across."[25]

In their efforts to teach, weathercasters must guard against the stuffy, formal delivery that went out of favor decades ago. A survey of television weathercasters in 1985 found that 92 percent favored a "relaxed, casual" approach in their weather shows. Only 7 percent opted for a "technical, scientific" style, while the remainder admitted their preference for a humorous weathercast.[26]

"It took me thirty-five years to educate the people," says Marcia Yockey of her career at WFIE and WTVW in Evansville, Indiana. Yockey found it best not to call attention to her efforts: "You don't ever want [viewers] to know you're educating them.... But if you sneak it in on them, then they can't live without it."[27]

Many weather anchors prefer to instruct through simple elaboration on a day's weather events. For example, a heat wave can provide an opportunity to discuss high-pressure cells and their ability to block other weather systems' progress. The variable climate of Salt Lake City gave Rebecca

Reheis ample material for viewers of KTVX. "Whenever an [unusual weather] event occurs, we'll try to whip up a graphic so that people can understand and look for what we're talking about... I want people to walk away saying, 'I get it!' Weather's something that happens every single day, yet hardly anyone knows how it occurs or why it occurs."

Time is the main limit to the educational efforts of Reheis and her colleagues. "On the late show, I get three or three and a half minutes. There's not a lot you can do. Plus, we cover five states...."[28]

Weathercast Geography

Some parts of the United States work against the detailed, informative weathercast just by their location. In Los Angeles, where the vast majority of days are sunny and placid, comic weathercasters far outnumber those with a serious approach. The humorous tone in Los Angeles weather is so ingrained that in 1985, a professional comedian was tapped for KNBC's prime-time weather spot.[29]

In some midwestern or coastal cities, such an approach would be heresy. These places depend upon weather for agriculture or recreation; they must also contend with deadly storms. In such markets, the serious weathercast is more a tradition than a trend. The prevailing standard tends to make any attempt at a lighthearted weather segment look foolish.

In a 1973 *TV Guide* article, Joe Witte (then of Seattle's KING and more recently on "NBC News at Sunrise") gave a succinct defense of the serious approach to weathercasting.

> In my estimation, viewers see nothing funny about weather, especially in Seattle where we get 35 inches of rain a year. It affects farming, logging, fishing and recreation. I don't believe in a lot of technical talk when giving weather news, but I don't believe in clowning, either....[30]

One good example of a weather-conscious television market is Omaha, at the northern end of Tornado Alley and prone to blizzards as well. All three of Omaha's network affiliates had Doppler radar by the late 1980s (these radars are excellent for severe-weather coverage but expensive). At that time, five of the market's seven weathercasters were degreed meteorologists, and one of the remaining two had an AMS seal of approval. The presence of Offutt Air Force Base near Omaha, with its large contingent of meteorologists, ensures a stream of scientifically-qualified talent for local television.

And by all accounts, the devotion to weather on Omaha television has paid off. A 1975 tornado produced $140 million in damage, one of the country's largest tolls to that date from a single twister, but only three deaths. The National Weather Service in Omaha had issued timely warnings that were promptly broadcast on local media.

While geography helps encourage serious weathercasts, it's not enough to ensure them. Kansas City — only 200 miles south of Omaha and a much larger population center — had only one Doppler radar among its three major stations in the late 1980s, and meteorologists have long been in the minority among Kansas City weathercasters.

What accounts for such differences? Beyond local idiosyncrasies, it seems that an early commitment to serious weather coverage by at least one station in a market can set the precedent for decades to come. Geography and sensitive station management combined to make two stations leaders in the art of serious weathercasting. WKY (now KTVY) in Oklahoma City and WTVT in Tampa were founded amid the local threats of tornadoes and hurricanes, respectively. The stations, both owned by the Oklahoma Publishing Company during the 1950s, became two of the country's first to install radar. WKY pushed severe-weather coverage into a new era by telecasting the country's first tornado warning, while WTVT enhanced its hurricane reporting by pioneering regular satellite pictures in 1966. Viewers in both cities continued to enjoy in-depth weather coverage through the 1980s.

IN THE COMMUNITY

One element of style can be found among humorous and noncomic weathercasters alike: outreach to the audience. Public service has long been a mainstay of local programming, because of the Federal Communication Commission's early requirement for such service as part of its licensing regulations. Yet while that FCC requirement was loosened in the 1980s, weathercasters' on- and off-the-air bids for public attention have continued to grow.

Many of the first public-relations gimmicks by weathercasters involved children. Bill Keene, of Los Angeles' KNXT, earned nationwide attention for his "School-O-Meter," a graphic relating Keene's forecast to the clothing school kids should wear the next day. (The idea, Keene told *TV Guide,* was a response to "The Mickey Mouse Club," his on-air competition: "I was getting killed in the ratings. I had to do something to attract mothers.") Keene also involved children more directly by soliciting their weather-related artwork, showing one such illustration each night. At one point in the early 1970s, Keene had a backlog of over a thousand illustrations for display.[31] Another weathercaster who used this technique in the 1980s was Guy Sharpe on Atlanta's WXIA.[32]

Of course, adults enjoy recognition on television as much as youngsters.

Playing host to a troop of Girl Scouts, Joe Denardo (WTAE, Pittsburgh) demonstrates the community involvement often expected of weathercasters. (Courtesy WTAE)

Moreover, thousands of adults follow the weather on their own through home observing stations. These elements played into a rapid growth in "weather watcher" clubs, composed of viewers who phone in daily weather reports to be compiled on a special local map. Boston's Don Kent formed a group of several dozen ham-radio operators, the New England Weather Net, in the 1950s for his WBZ weathercasts. Their observations ranged from temperature, sky cover, and wind to seasonal phenomena such as blooming plants and fall foliage.[33]

Restrictions on graphics and labor kept the weather-watcher idea limited through the 1970s to a few big-city stations, such as KSTP in Minneapolis. But in the next decade, technology gave the concept a boost. Telephone-answering machines and computer modems allowed viewers to make their reports without distracting station personnel. Plotting 30 or 40 such observations was easier for weathercasters with the help of computers. Recognizing the trend, the American Association of Weather Observers (AAWO) began acknowledging such television observer networks in the early 1980s. Stations represented in the AAWO by 1987 included KTVI (St. Louis), WDIV (Detroit), WSPA (Spartanburg, S.C.), KTHI (Fargo, N.D.), and WITI (Milwaukee).

Weather literature was another way for stations to enhance their public profile. A common technique in the 1980s was to merchandise such products through restaurants, supermarkets, and the like. Countless grocery bags were emblazoned with severe-weather tips and the faces of local weathercasters. Almanacs and severe-weather guides were also popular, distributed free or at a nominal cost. Jacksonville's WJXT published over 10,000 "Weather Guides" annually in the 1980s. Perhaps a million such booklets go from various stations to viewers each year, giving the latter a tangible link to the weathercaster they watch nightly.

NEITHER WIND, NOR SNOW, NOR RAIN...

Among the many scornful stereotypes of weather forecasters is that of the bright, well-meaning soothsayer hunched over maps, predicting sunshine even as the raindrops fall outside his door. One way to counter this notion is by putting the weathercast outdoors — the ultimate community involvement.

This approach was difficult in the 1950s when television cameras were bulky machines not easily transported outside a studio. Some stations did *simulate* outdoor weather in the early days, though. Bud Kraeling did weathercasts on Minneapolis' WCCO in 1951–1961 from the "Shell Weather Tower," a studio enclosure meant to resemble a Shell Oil platform. Each segment opened with film of a real oil derrick, with the camera zooming to the top and then dissolving to the indoor weather set. Kraeling enhanced the illusion by wearing a Shell uniform and placing his weather maps on the back of Shell products.[34]

As broadcast equipment improved, more and more weather anchors took an occasional bona fide venture off the weather set. By the mid-1980s, some local and national weathercasters seemed to spend more air time outside than inside their studios. In particular, network morning shows used their plentiful travel funds and remote-video facilities to send their personnel wherever weather — or other — news was happening. On one Friday morning in 1985, ABC's Dave Murray and CBS's Steve Baskerville did their weather spots from a St. Louis carnival, while NBC's Willard Scott broadcast from Greenville, S.C., at a hot-air balloon festival.[35]

Few local stations have the resources for such globetrotting, yet most can afford remote shots from events or locations within their viewing area. Computerized maps can assist these efforts. Typically, a weather anchor briefs himself beforehand, then goes to a remote site and does the show while referring to a monitor that shows the relevant weather data (which the audience also sees).

Remote weathercasts can be highly dramatic. John Coleman did one segment for Chicago's WLS perched on a beam atop the 110-story Sears Tower, which was then under construction. His explanation for viewers: "I am looking out on the western horizon to try to find that front I've been predicting the last few days."[36]

Often, the drama is produced by weather itself. Rebecca Reheis took her KTVX weathercasts outdoors when Salt Lake City experienced "interesting" weather. "It's a segment I call 'Weather to Go.' The more severe the weather, the better it is. . . . In December [1988], we had 110-mile-an-hour winds, and I was literally blown out of the camera frame."[37] Comical weathercasters also use the outdoors for effect. Lloyd Lindsay Young delivered an Idaho Falls segment wearing only a swimsuit as a snowstorm raged around him.[38]

While many local stations do an occasional weather segment outside, only a few make outdoor weather a regular feature. In Minneapolis, Syracuse, Buffalo, and Pittsburgh, viewers have seen the weather presented amid all kinds of weather. Dennis Bowman, of Pittsburgh's WPXI, broadcasts on the station roof, sheltered by a canopy in case of rain. A chromakey setup enables Bowman to gesture at maps, using a blank wall. The rooftop affords Bowman and his audience a 40-mile view on clear days, and only the threat of lightning brings the Bowman show indoors. "We have spectacular sunset shots," says Bowman.[39]

Weathercasting outside is one way to illustrate local variations in climate. In San Francisco, where such variations are extreme, Mark Thompson specializes in "Neighborhood Weather." Human interest is added to Thompson's segments when he does weather for KRON from the yards and homes of Bay Area residents. The generally mild conditions in San Francisco allow "Neighborhood Weather" to be a year-round feature.

Should outdoor weather fail to boost ratings enough, one gimmick seems to be an inexpensive, simple, surefire way to liven up weathercasts. Don Noe (while in Green Bay, Wisconsin), John Coleman, and Lloyd Lindsay Young have all delivered weather segments while standing on their heads. Was any more ever asked of Walter Cronkite or David Brinkley?

4

Television and the Weather Service

"Public-private partnership" became a catchphrase in the 1980s as the United States government tightened its domestic-spending habits. Private enterprise was increasingly tapped to perform many of the duties formerly handled by federal agencies, from running concession stands in national parks to operating mass-transit systems.

In promoting these ideas, fans of the public-private mixture overlooked one of the best examples of cooperation between government and business. Television weather is a near-perfect illustration of how one federal unit and several hundred private companies can collaborate to bring information to the public. Although a good share, perhaps a majority, of television weathercasters are well enough trained in meteorology to issue their own forecasts, they and their colleagues would be lost without the warnings, outlooks, and observations collected and distributed by the National Weather Service.* Conversely, many of the Weather Service's products would be useless if not promptly broadcast through the media.

The NWS-television relationship hasn't been without occasional storminess. Some weathercasters routinely give the NWS forecast word for word and pass it off as their own. Others regularly buck the NWS party line, even in severe-weather situations, adding to a mishmash of warnings and outlooks. On the whole, though, weather forecasting is one of those rare areas in which the interaction between government and media has been cooperative instead of contentious.

---

*The service operated as part of the U.S. Army's Signal Service from its establishment in 1870 through 1891. It was then renamed the U.S. Weather Bureau and transferred to the Department of Agriculture. In 1940, the bureau was assigned to the Department of Commerce, and in 1970, its original name — the National Weather Service — was restored. In this chapter, the names Weather Bureau (or WB) and Weather Service (or NWS) are used according to the era being discussed.

THE FIRST FORECASTS: A BRIEF NWS HISTORY

While individuals had been keeping weather records since the United States was founded, it was the invention of the telegraph in 1837 that made a national weather service feasible. Reports could now be compiled in enough time to track weather systems and issue forecasts based on the calculated motion. The loss of several thousand sailors in storms on the Great Lakes during the late 1860s prompted Congress to act on the suggestions of many and create an agency for storm monitoring and prediction. Within a few years of its 1870 formation, the National Weather Service was providing regular outlooks from its Washington office and publishing weekly and monthly weather summaries.

Telegraphy had its limitations as a means of transmitting weather data. Lines broke during storms, just when information was most needed. Coding and decoding slowed the forecast process. Perhaps most crucially, the relaying of important information could be hindered by a single recipient. One frost warning issued for Madison, Wisconsin, in the 1880s failed to save the region's tobacco crop because the local telegraph operator did not pass on the Weather Service advisory.[1]

No wonder, then, that the Weather Bureau was the first government agency to express an interest in radio. In 1900, the bureau hired Aubrey Fessender from Western University (later the University of Pittsburgh) to investigate the feasibility of transmitting weather details by "wireless." Fessender succeeded in building several radio stations, but direct Weather Bureau subsidizing of radio soon ended at the behest of President Theodore Roosevelt.[2]

Interaction continued, though, between the bureau and radio. As early as 1902, the U.S. Coast Guard transmitted Weather Bureau information and accepted observations from ships on the Great Lakes and the Atlantic Ocean. In the 1910s, the focus shifted to bureau collaboration with experimental stations in the Midwest (usually operated by universities). Weather data were relayed to nine amateur radio operators throughout North Dakota by the state university beginning in 1914.[3] At the University of Wisconsin, Weather Bureau forecasts and market reports were the first regular feature of station 9XM in 1921.[4]

In late 1922 and 1923, the new medium began to grow far faster than observers could have predicted. The U.S. Department of Agriculture was at that time granting stations permission to broadcast market or weather reports. In June 1922, only 20 of the nation's 36 commercial stations were licensed to transmit Weather Bureau forecasts. "The ultimate plan in mind will provide for the distribution on fixed schedules of weather forecasts and warnings from at least one radio station in each state," wrote Edgar Calvert in 1921.[5] It took less than two years for Calvert's "ultimate plan" to be eclipsed: all 140 stations existing in January 1923 were certified for weather-casts, covering most states.[6] Not all of these stations relied completely on the Weather Bureau for information. New York's first radio weathercast, transmitted August 3, 1922, by WBAY (later WEAF), featured six minutes of observations collected by AT&T employees from Pittsburgh to San Francisco.[7]

With radio's continuing growth in the late 1920s and 1930s came more variety in weathercasting. A hallmark of this period was the creation of flexible links between radio stations and local Weather Bureau offices. These enabled stations to cover specific local threats in depth rather than simply passing along standard forecasts. One example was the arrangement between KFI in Los Angeles and the L.A. Weather Bureau. During winter and spring, KFI broadcast a nightly frost-warning advisory (provided by the Weather Bureau) giving the likelihood in each of several zones of a frost that could damage citrus crops.[8]

The KFI broadcasts illustrate how closely information on weather and on agriculture was coupled in the 1930s, even on big-city stations. This developed partially because regular newscasts were absent on most stations. Radio news as a genre didn't develop until the later 1930s, at which time weathercasting began to fall into its domain. Even then, strong ties continued between radio weather and the Weather Bureau. A number of stations made time for regular appearances by bureau forecasters: for ex-ample, John Murphy of the Norfolk Weather Bureau gave noontime reports on WTAR.[9] Some 70 stations across the United States featured Weather Bureau staff on their programming by 1940. A bureau committee reported that year to the secretary of agriculture that most of these arrange-ments worked well and asserted that the WB should "considerably extend and improve its own broadcasting and educational service."[10] With this in mind, the Bureau established a broadcasting training program in its Wash-ington, D.C., headquarters, aimed at familiarizing staff with the pro-cedures used in radio.

Meanwhile, a few private meteorologists such as Jim Fidler started radio careers. Though people like Fidler might have seen the use of govern-ment employees on radio as unfair competition, no major protests were lodged. (The outcome was to be different once the Weather Bureau got in-volved in the far more competitive world of television.)

Even at this early point, some of the private radio weathercasters took the liberty of deviating from the official bureau forecasts. Jim Fidler described his approach in a 1938 article for the *Bulletin of the American Meteorological Society:*

> Many times the author has predicted storms in advance of the first re-ports on the news service teletypes.... It is not implied that such [advance

predictions] can possibly rival or take the place of the regular 12- to 36-hr
forecasts of such organizations as the Weather Bureau. . . .

The Weather Bureau forecasters are not free to make use of all the information that is available to the independent observer. This brings us to a
point that must be guarded most carefully. . . . The weather man who
broadcasts the weather other than the verbatim reading of the official
reports should be qualified for the assignment.[11]

Fidler anticipated a concern of the TV era—the misinterpretation of
Weather Service material by weathercasters without training in meteorology. A knowledgeable weather anchor can often improve on NWS forecasts by taking into account changes in conditions between the forecast's
issuance and the weathercast. Yet, by the same token, a misinformed person may attempt to explain the official forecast with faulty reasoning or
misused jargon. Transcripts show that Fidler himself carefully identified
the sources of all information used in his weathercasts, separating Weather
Bureau outlooks from his own.

THE BUREAU KICKS OFF TELEVISION

Just as it had devoted resources to radio during that medium's fledgling
period, the Weather Bureau saw television's potential in the 1940s and
directed its energy accordingly. The bureau's broadcasting unit branched
into television in 1947 and began regular telecasts on the DuMont network
in late 1947 (the DuMont stations were WTTG, Washington; WMAR,
Baltimore; WFIL, Philadelphia; and WABD, New York). After yielding a
number of insights into the potential and problems of television, the experiment ended in 1948 with some discouragement at the medium's "static"
qualities.[12]

However, private weathercasting expanded into television just as the
Weather Bureau retrenched. An observer in 1949, profiling Louis Allen on
Washington's WNBW, noted: "There are several other non–Weather
Bureau meteorologists operating TV weather programs on somewhat the
same basis as Allen does. . . . The WB supplies them the charts and is otherwise helpful within its practical limits."[13] Those limits proved more restric-
tive in some cities than in others. Television stations with weather wire and
a skilled weathercaster could decipher the teletyped information and create
their own weather maps. Until the mid-1950s, though, teletype links to the
Weather Bureau were hard to come by, due to bureau concerns over their
misuse. To depict weather without this coded data, completed maps had to
be secured from a local Weather Bureau office, and these were not necessarily located near television stations. (Frank Field, at New York's WNBC
since 1957, was lucky; New York's bureau was downstairs from WNBC

The U.S. Weather Bureau first delved into television broadcasting in the late 1940s. Jim Fidler stands before a map used in the bureau's experimental broadcasts on several East Coast stations. (Courtesy Jim Fidler)

studios in Manhattan's Rockefeller Center, making it easy for Field to check data within a few minutes of airtime if necessary.)[14]

POLICY PROBLEMS

The Weather Bureau's laissez-faire policy of allowing its personnel to appear on commercial media met its first solid resistance in 1954. Years of radio appearances had caused no controversy, and the logistics of television seemed to provide a built-in limit to Weather Bureau involvement: live broadcasts from a bureau office were then technically difficult and time-consuming. Still, the presence of a single bureau employee on network television was enough to draw fire from two different sources.

Jim Fidler and "Today"

The offending weathercaster was none other than radio veteran Jim Fidler. Employed for years by private media, he joined the Weather Bureau broadcast unit in the late 1940s and appeared on the bureau's experimental weathercasts in 1947–1948. In January 1952, Fidler was tapped by NBC's fledgling morning program, "Today." The arrangement was simple: Three times during each program, "Today" host Dave Garroway phoned Fidler at his Weather Bureau office in Washington. Fidler provided weather details in a 2½-minute period as Garroway referred to a national map on camera. Another Weather Bureau meteorologist substituted for Fidler an average of three days a month.[15] Though Fidler never appeared on camera, his voice transmissions were clearly a regular part of "Today."

On April 28, 1954, the U.S. House of Representatives Select Committee on Small Business notified the Department of Commerce that a complaint had been lodged against Fidler's appearances on "Today." That complaint read in part:

> ... Unfair competition by the U.S. Weather Bureau is seriously hampering my efforts to build a private meteorological practice in the realm of commercial television....
>
> My experiences indicate that television management wants to use Weather Bureau employees for two reasons:
>
> 1. Their services are free (or nominal), and their performances can thus be sold to advertisers at 100 percent profit.
>
> 2. Appearances by persons representing the government serves [sic] as a tacit endorsement of sponsors' products.
>
> Television management wants free, low-cost meteorologists, and the Weather Bureau supplies them.[16]

These arguments were difficult to refute, yet the Weather Bureau made an immediate attempt to do so. On May 4, bureau Director F. W. Reichelderfer responded point-by-point to questions from the Committee on Small Business. He emphasized that no Weather Bureau employees were making regular appearances on local television (although one-time guest spots were frequent).[17] Still, many WB personnel had done regular radio programs for years. In that light, the policy against regular television work seemed inconsistent, and in Fidler's case, the policy was clearly unenforced.

Reichelderfer addressed this contradiction by noting the voice-only nature of Fidler's participation in "Today" (making it similar to radio work) and the Weather Bureau's mandate to "gather and publish" weather information as widely as possible.

> This participation has been authorized as part of the Weather Bureau's regular responsibility of disseminating timely weather information to the

general public. It is analogous to the information that any person could obtain from the Weather Bureau by telephone but through cooperation with the network program the Bureau is thus enabled to reach hundreds of thousands of people.... No commercial sponsorship or advertising is involved.[18]

Though Fidler himself did not mention sponsors' names, NBC often placed advertising logos above the weather map shown on camera while Fidler talked.

Reichelderfer's comments might have put the matter to rest had there not been another complaint regarding "Today," this one from the American Federation of Television and Radio Artists (AFTRA). In June 1954, AFTRA notified the House Committee on Small Business of its displeasure regarding Fidler's unpaid appearances on "Today." AFTRA's position was that Fidler and any other Weather Bureau employees appearing regularly on commercial television should be considered performers subject to union jurisdiction and paid at union rates.[19] However, Fidler and his substitute received no pay from NBC for their "Today" work; it was considered part of their government-salaried duties. To receive external pay for such work would pose a different set of ethical problems.

The cumulative pressure of these criticisms brought the end of routine Weather Bureau ventures into commercial television. On August 25, 1954, F. W. Reichelderfer issued a directive to Weather Bureau employees, forbidding any regular appearances "either by voice or by person" on commercial television shows. Two important exceptions were maintained: Bureau personnel could make guest appearances on commercial television, and they could use any medium necessary in extreme weather situations.[20]

While it effectively closed the saga of "Today" and Jim Fidler (whose appearances on the show had actually ended two months earlier), the new policy wasn't perfect. Fidler's "Today" contribution, little different from that to a radio show, was prohibited. Yet Weather Bureau forecasters were allowed to maintain their regular spots on commercial radio and noncommercial television.[21] Since nobody had complained about such appearances, the bureau was inclined to continue permitting them, even at the cost of inconsistency.

The Evolution of Policy

After the brief Jim Fidler–"Today" controversy, a remarkably long period of harmonious interaction ensued between the Weather Bureau and television stations. Problems in the relationship had been smoothed over to nearly everyone's satisfaction. Between 1954 and 1970, television weather grew from infancy to maturity with increasingly stable links to the Bureau.

In the 1970s, though, concern grew over loopholes in the Weather Bureau's radio-television policy. The first formal statement of the guidelines drawn up in 1954 appeared in 1970, just before creation of the National Oceanic and Atmospheric Administration (NOAA, encompassing the renamed National Weather Service). Section 27-13 of the first *NOAA Directives Manual* essentially restated the distinction between regular radio and regular television appearances by NWS employees, encouraging the former but forbidding the latter.[22]

That dichotomy weakened in 1972 following political pressure. Topeka's WTSB had begun regular telecasts of local radar displays, coupled with the voice of a Topeka NWS employee analyzing the radar image. NOAA informed the station that such transmissions were against policy. The WTSB station manager contacted U.S. Senator James Pearson, who in turn protested to NOAA that the agency's media policy discriminated against television stations in favor of radio.[23]

In apparent agreement with Senator Pearson, NOAA changed its policy in August 1972 to allow a specific exception to the no-television-appearance rule: television stations could now broadcast the prerecorded voice of a Weather Service employee commenting on radar images. Such tapes had to be available to all television stations by telephone, thus preventing the exclusiveness of Jim Fidler's arrangement with NBC.[24]

NOAA's policy became even more complicated when the specific exception of 1972 became a general rule revision in 1973.[25] The new guidelines for both radio and television, as reiterated in 1975, stated: "Regular direct voice transmission originating in a NOAA office, live or recorded, using the voice of a NOAA employee, are permitted and are encouraged, especially during periods involving natural hazards." What had become of the prohibition of regular television work? "Routine personal appearances" on television were forbidden in the same set of guidelines.[26] The key word is *appearances:* NOAA was now interpreting voice-only television work as separate from on-camera work. Ironically, NOAA had now legitimized, in letter if not in spirit, the same sort of television position Jim Fidler had been forced to relinquish.

In practice, Weather Service employees did not rush to the phones for regular television voice-overs. The mid-1970s was a period of increasing sophistication in television weather. More weathercasters were emphasizing their independence from NWS forecasts. The demand for NWS "voice transmissions" was thus low, and Weather Service employees may have been leery of such work after two decades of its being prohibited. In any case, their newfound freedom was short-lived, as NOAA rescinded the distinction between vocal and on-camera television appearances in 1978.[27]

Television Weather Goes Public

One highly successful government venture into television prompted a different rule change in 1975. "Aviation Weather," a Maryland public-television program, featured Federal Aviation Administration employees giving detailed weather summaries (see Chapter 8). After the program became successful, NOAA considered supplying its own meteorologists for the show. Since "Aviation Weather" was primarily government-sponsored, it seemed to carry little risk of conflict of interest. NOAA thus rewrote its television policy to allow "routine personal appearances on *non-commercial* [NOAA's emphasis] public broadcasting television in environmental information programs" if such work was part of "official NOAA duties." Regular appearances on *commercial* television were still off-limits.[28]

That distinction solved the "Aviation Weather" problem until 1978 when the show was reincarnated as "A.M. Weather" and began appearing on over 150 public-television outlets. In November of that year, New York's public station, WNET, had not yet picked up "A.M. Weather." Noting the show's popularity elsewhere, WCBS, a commercial station in New York, filed a request with NOAA to broadcast "A.M. Weather" as long as WNET declined the program.[29] NOAA turned down WCBS's request but noted that its contact with the Maryland Center for Public Broadcasting did not expressly forbid the rebroadcast of "A.M. Weather" segments on commercial television.[30]

Anticipating more such requests, NOAA formed a study team in June 1980 to decide whether "A.M. Weather" should be released to *every* commercial station requesting it. NOAA's thinking was that any service partially funded by the government should be equally available to any qualified user, much as National Weather Service data itself is. Moreover, distributing "A.M. Weather" more widely would not result in major added expense.

After interviewing managers at 14 radio and television stations, the study team found widespread satisfaction with NOAA's role as an information source and little demand for change. The team thus voted to continue NOAA's ban on routine commercial-television appearances by its employees. At the same time (somewhat paradoxically), it recommended the release of "A.M. Weather" to commercial stations "if such utilization were in the interest of NOAA, were equally available to all, were desired by the commercial broadcasters, and were considered by NOAA management not to be in competition with the private sector." In the study team's eyes, "A.M. Weather" posed no threat to commercial outlets since it could be used by any or all of them, whereas individual weathercasts could not be feasibly provided by the Weather Service to every station in every market. The team's suggestions went unheeded, though: NOAA decided to maintain its policy of distributing "A.M. Weather" only to public stations.[31]

That 1981 decision began another period of unusual quiet in NWS-television relations. Throughout the Reagan presidency, private initiatives were encouraged in place of government intervention. Suggesting any added involvement from the NWS in weathercasting was hardly fashionable in this decade of budget-cutting. The decade ended with no further shifts in the NOAA radio-television policy. Once again, the Weather Service had decided to leave television weathercasting to the (television) professionals.

RADIO AND CABLE: A HIT AND A MISS

Aside from various policy shifts on commercial-television involvement, the NWS kept itself in the media business in other ways. One of these ventures proved a modest success, while another was outdated by private initiative.

NOAA Weather Radio

With television dominating radio by the 1960s, the time hardly seemed ripe for a network of government radio stations broadcasting nonstop weather data. Yet NOAA Weather Radio quickly filled a neglected niche. Millions of radios tuned to the NOAA VHF frequencies (near 162.5 Mhz) were sold, and by 1986 three-quarters of the United States populace could pick up Weather Service broadcasts.[32]

The roots of NOAA Weather Radio lie in a public accustomed to having weather information available at its fingertips. For decades, that role was filled by Weather Bureau telephone services. As early as 1904, some 60,000 farmers in Ohio were obtaining daily weather reports by telephone. By 1939, residents of New York could dial a prerecorded message, updated frequently, that gave local weather conditions and the forecast.[33]

Such services proved too popular for their own good. The largest Weather Bureau offices were swamped with thousands of calls each day, jamming phone lines. At the same time, many people wanted more than the routine information given. Boaters, campers, and others sought details beyond the scope of a one-minute recording. The Federal Aviation Administration (FAA) provided radio weather tailored to aviators, but the details and terminology were often irrelevant for other listeners.

The solution devised by ESSA (the Environmental Science Services Administration, NOAA's predecessor) in the 1960s was to begin 24-hour weather broadcasts on radio. These featured prerecorded Weather Bureau personnel giving local conditions and forecasts, much like the ongoing phone service but with the information recycled about every five minutes. Special advisories were tailored for marine interests, agriculture, and the like. Regular programming was suspended for timely bulletins in the event of severe weather.

Growth of the weather-radio network was at first sporadic. Nineteen cities were served by 1969, most of them on the United States coastlines or in the Midwest.[34] In the 1970s, though, the program took off. Nearly 100 stations were on the air by 1977,[35] and over 100 more were being planned. With an average transmitting range of around 40 miles, some 350 NOAA Weather Radio stations were reaching most United States population centers of consequence by the mid-1980s.[36]

Private enterprise gained from the NOAA network as well. Radio manufacturers built receivers exclusively designed for the Weather Service broadcasts. Many of these featured "tone alerts," an inventive way to warn of severe weather. In the event of a tornado warning, hurricane watch, or other weather alert, NOAA stations broadcast a special high-pitched siren for a few seconds preceding the urgent weather announcement. Radios with the tone-alert capacity could be placed on a setting that would broadcast only such an alarm, otherwise remaining silent. The feature gave schools, hospitals, and other institutions a simple way to monitor dangerous weather without having to sift through other information. Even mass media found NOAA Weather Radio useful; some Midwest radio stations worked out agreements with NOAA to "simulcast" severe-weather bulletins directly from the Weather Radio.[37]

NOAA Weather Radio's wide coverage and acceptance made it suitable for a much different kind of warning as well. The network was designated in 1975 as the sole government medium for transmitting information to private homes on nuclear attack.[38]

No-Frills Cable

Preceding the growth of cable television into a nationwide source of weather data (see Chapter 8) were experiments in providing local weather details via cable. Though private companies oversaw the creation of most such systems, their information usually came undiluted from the NWS.

Planners of community-access television (CATV, as cable systems were then called) found weather a helpful way to fill out empty channels. The Hobbs (N.M.) Television Company set up its own observing station for continuous broadcast. Dial displays of wind speed, temperature, pressure, and the like were rotated on camera at five-second intervals by a set of automated rotating mirrors. Audio came from the local FAA broadcasts; in other cities, FM stations provided background music.[39]

Electronics entered the picture by 1970. Character generators could now produce text giving weather conditions as well as forecasts and advisories from the National Weather Service. At the same time, cable television itself was growing in popularity, and NOAA Weather Radio was expanding rapidly. These ingredients came together in the early 1970s to produce 24-hour cable weather in Galveston, New Orleans, Tampa, and other coastal cities served by the NOAA network. Such coverage included live radar images and videotext with a Weather Radio voice-over.[40]

Could even better cable weather be produced with help from the Weather Service? That question was studied through a CATV experiment in Great Falls, Montana, that spanned four months in late 1973. The Great Falls branch of TelePrompter Cable TV joined the Weather Service in financing and constructing a weather studio of sorts at the Great Falls NWS office. Personnel there created five minutes of weather programming every half hour, including hand-produced maps and a voice-over. The other 50 minutes of each broadcast hour was filled with videotext weather information and FM music.[41]

Public reaction seemed favorable to the half-hourly weathercasts (though some businesses using the FM background music complained about the five-minute NWS interruptions). Subscriptions to the Great Falls TelePrompter service increased from 10,000 to 12,000 over the test period, and the Weather Service logged many calls of concern during a brief equipment failure. Still, yearly expenses of such a system were estimated at $50,000, aside from start-up costs and other contingencies. NOAA's interim report found these figures too high for a nationwide network of Great Falls–type coverage.[42]

As it turned out, the late 1970s and early 1980s saw a nationwide boom in cable television and formation of The Weather Channel. That single outlet of information quickly became better equipped to provide 24-hour cable weather than any number of local Weather Service offices could have been.

WHOSE FORECAST IS IT?

One point of concern in the meteorological community for decades has been the appropriate degree of acknowledgement television stations should give to the National Weather Service for supplying data, maps, and forecasts. While television weather had relied on government products from the start, there was no denying that more information was being supplied each year. Weather wire made it to many stations by the late 1950s; facsimile transmissions of NWS maps grew wildly during the 1960s; satellite photos became more common at the same time; and hookups to NWS radar began by 1970. Private contractors created and sold the equipment for these data sources, but the data were all courtesy of the government.

Few viewers of television weather in the 1960s or the 1980s knew that simple fact. The average weathercaster presented each day's government outlook as simply "the forecast," "our forecast," or even "my forecast." If the NWS ever received mention, it typically came only for weather observations; for example, "the Weather Service got one-point-four-five inches of rain this morning." Rare was the weathercaster who gave scrupulous credit to the service for map positions, extended outlooks, and the like, as Jim Fidler did in his radio weather of the 1930s.

One clear reason for the lack of credit is television's stinginess with time. With only two or three minutes per weathercast, a major chunk of the program could be lost if proper credit was given. Such a constant, repetitive reminder might also detract from the more changeable and significant weather data. Still, the collective egos of television stations are perhaps a greater block to acknowledging help from the Weather Bureau. By hiring meteorologists or purchasing high-tech equipment, stations hope to enhance their impression of authority in weather matters. It wouldn't help that cause to admit that the vast majority of weathercast information comes directly from the government.

The study group formed by NOAA in 1980 to evaluate television-radio policy noted station managers' reluctance to give the Weather Service its proper due.

> Those [radio] stations that do not use a private meteorologist were quick to point out that they always acknowledge the NWS as the source of the data and forecasts they broadcast.[*] The stations that use or have a private meteorologist were somewhat more evasive in their answer.... They did not want to convey the thought to their audience that they were not doing something unique and special. They want to convey the idea that their meteorologist is the best and therefore their station is the best for having him.[43]

When severe weather strikes, the issue of concordance between the Weather Service and media intensifies. Social scientists have found that conflicting information regarding an imminent natural hazard tends to slow the recipients' response. While there is no explicit ban on television or radio outlets' issuing their own "tornado warnings" or "flash-flood watches," the NWS has strongly discouraged this practice for decades. One result is the tendency for radio announcers to read weather bulletins verbatim, crediting the Weather Service. Likewise, television usually displays severe-weather information in the exact NWS format. Weathercasters breaking into programming for especially critical warnings might skip the NWS credit, but the overwhelming consensus is to stick with the government's word in dangerous weather.

---

*Radio stations are much more likely than television stations to give the NWS explicit credit for a forecast, often by such statements as "The National Weather Service forecast for tonight is . . ."

Facsimile lines bring maps and charts from the National Weather Service to hundreds of television stations. George Winterling (WJXT, Jacksonville) used such maps extensively in 1975, before computer graphics arrived. (Courtesy WJXT)

A few well-trained weathercasters step over that invisible line on occasion, often generating heated reactions among colleagues. In hurricane coverage, New Orleans' Nash Roberts became a local legend for publicly disagreeing with the National Hurricane Center. Although he retired from regular weathercasting on WWL in 1980, Roberts returned to the air during hurricane threats through the following decade. His 40 years in hurricane research and prediction gave him the confidence to spot trends in storm behavior and report them on-air before official sources had time to issue a complete update. When Roberts computed and announced his own coordinates one night for 1985's Hurricane Elena, competing weathercasters were up in arms, making such remarks on the air as "There is no way anybody else at any other TV station can have more accurate information [than the official reports]" and "The official coordinates are the only ones you'll get from us." Yet Roberts earned praise from the major New Orleans newspaper: "Nash Roberts is still the most reliable weatherman in the city. . . . He dilutes hurricane panic with information."[44]

Another maverick, Gary England of Oklahoma City's KWTV, has received both praise and criticism for his handling of tornadoes. Though the Oklahoma City NWS is an acknowledged leader in severe-storm warnings,

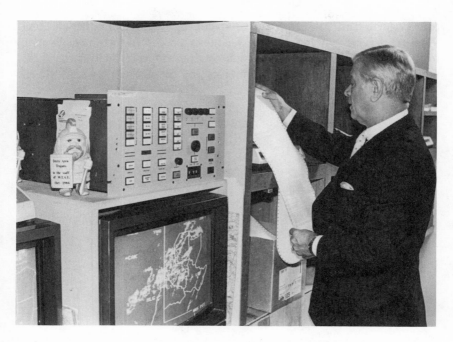

Joe Denardo (WTAE, Pittsburgh) examines output from the Pennsylvania weather wire, a valuable data source. To his left is another helpful aid: color-radar data from Pittsburgh's National Weather Service radar. (Courtesy WTAE)

England's Doppler radar is comparable with the best Weather Service equipment for tornado detection. On occasion, England has noted the possibility of tornadoes before a relevant NWS statement was issued. His warning in May 1983 for Ada, Oklahoma, reportedly preceded tornado damage by 20 minutes and the NWS warning by several minutes. England's independence has created some conflict with the local Weather Service.[45]

Severe weather is the most dramatic focus of dissonance between television and the National Weather Service, but everyday forecasts can show a difference as well. One study of Indianapolis weathercasts from October 1980 found considerable disagreement between the three major stations' nightly outlooks, implying some independence from the NWS. Most variations were minor; for example, stations' overnight-low predictions were seldom identical but usually fell within a five-degree range. Discrepancies were larger in rain forecasts and long-term outlooks.[46] Other research has shown a similar pattern; stations rarely stick to every number from a Weather Service outlook, but drastic deviations from the government line are just as rare.

Perhaps that typifies the relationship between weathercasters and their federal colleagues. Beyond the occasional bickering, television people seem to recognize and respect the untold contributions from the National Weather Service that go into each weather segment. In turn, though some in the NWS might criticize television weather, most treat it as the single most important link between themselves and the public they serve.

5

Technical Matters

Watching the weather outside is a simple matter. No special equipment is needed — other than a good view. Watching the weather on television is another matter, at least from the broadcaster's point of view. How can the vast range of weather conditions occurring across a large area — sleet, snow, heat, hail, or rain — be graphically summarized and depicted in a two-minute program? Some of the most refined technology ever used on television (or anywhere else) has been applied to that very question.[1]

Perhaps nothing about television weather in 40 years has changed more than the sheer look of it. Weathercasters still deliver their forecasts in tones ranging from the manic to the somber. Weather symbols haven't changed appreciably in four decades. Even the basic weathercast format is the same: local conditions, the national map, the state map, and tomorrow's outlook.

The contrast between then and now is truly amazing, though, when it comes to weather-program appearance. A typical early-1950s weathercast featured crude hand-drawn symbols for warm and cold fronts; most contemporary shows have the fronts flawlessly rendered by computer. The earliest radar displays showed nothing but diffuse blocks of white against a dingy grey background, in contrast to the brilliant colors and pinpoint definition of a 1980s radar.

Such progress has been expensive. At one time, station managers could get by with allotting only a pittance for weather production. The quickly evolving computer-graphics field now demands a substantial outlay for products that may well be obsolete after three to five years. Making an intelligent choice of visual aids for a weathercast requires as much knowledge of computers as of meteorology. Many stations opt for versatile graphics equipment that can operate far beyond the boundaries of weathercasting.

EARLY GRAPHICS

Popular wisdom has it that life was "simpler" in the 1950s. Certainly the tools of weathercasting at the time fit that description well. On-air personnel usually struggled with the barest minimum needed to convey a weather situation.

There was no electronic manipulation of displays, a process now taken for granted, even in smaller television markets. Instead of being stored in a computer, maps had to be drawn each day to the full dimensions needed, on the order of five by ten feet. Typically, a fixed background of geographic boundaries (states, counties, etc.) was superimposed with chalk drawings of high-pressure centers, cold fronts, and the like. The most elaborate setups used magnetic symbols to depict weather features such as clouds or sunshine. A common trick was to use symbols that respond to polarized light. As a specially designed light source rotated during the weathercast, the appearance of motion was created on these magnetic symbols. For example, rays of "sunshine" could be made to emanate from an artificial sun on the weather board. This early visual aid is still used in some markets.

For every map used during a 1950s weathercast, a separate background was needed (unless paper maps were posted atop each other and ripped off during the show). These multiple sets made for logistic headaches in going from one map to another, since only one or two cameras were used for a given broadcast. Yet another restriction on mapmaking was the failure of certain colors to broadcast well through the era's black-and-white cameras. Red, in particular, transmitted poorly. (This was used to the advantage of some early weathercasters who traced weather features in red before their show and then appeared to draw frontal positions from memory while on the air.)

Improvisation Rules

Ingenuity was clearly needed to keep a weathercast from sliding into the visual doldrums. Early weathercasters rose to the challenge by devising and improvising graphics, while often borrowing whatever seemed to work in other markets. One such technique that found its way into many a 1950s weather program was a see-through map. A pane of glass or thick plastic was permanently mounted in the studio, with geographic boundaries affixed to the plate. Armed with chalk or a crayon, the weathercaster stood behind the glass during the show, facing viewers, and drew weather features on the map while speaking. The drama of seeing weather unfold before one's eyes made this a popular device, used in such large markets as Chicago and Washington.

Cindy Dahl was one of Washington's most popular female weathercasters of the mid-1950s. At WTTG she drew map features on Plexiglas, a common gimmick during that period.

Presenting textual information was another challenge for early weathercasters. Severe-weather warnings had become standard, and stations sought ways to broadcast the bulletins without interrupting regular programs. The solution was to use "crawls," single lines of copy that run along the bottom of television screens, moving from right to left. In this precomputer era, crawl messages had to be typed onto long strips of plastic that were mounted on a large rotating drum. As light passed outward through the drum, the typed-out letters were illuminated; that image was then electronically superimposed onto regular broadcast signals. This low-tech method of airing weather and news crawls persisted through the 1960s on local and national television. NBC's "Today" used such crawls to carry the weather outlook for large cities (e.g., "Sunny in Seattle") during the show's five-minute breaks allotted for local programming.[2]

The Advent of Radar

By the mid-1950s, comical weathercasts were at their peak. Precious little attention was being paid to detailed weather information in most markets. In an effort to distinguish themselves, a few stations invested in a still-novel scientific instrument that provided visual appeal as well as hard information: radar (*r*adio *d*etection *a*nd *r*anging).

Radar burst onto the national scene during World War II as a potent means of detecting aircraft that were dozens or even hundreds of miles away. A radio transmitter, mounted in an upright rotating dish of metal several feet in width, sent out signals that struck objects and returned. By measuring the time needed for each signal to return, the distance of objects could be calculated. The rotating transmitter dish provided a 360-degree view of surroundings. Signals were displayed on a black-and-white screen.

One problem nagging radar's wartime users was the tendency of rainfall to appear on-screen, blocking returns from aircraft. This hindrance for aviation became a boon for weather forecasters after World War II. Radar signals of a certain wavelength were ideal for detecting precipitation. Rainfall or snowfall intensity could be discerned from the strength of returning signals on the display since heavier precipitation sent back a larger fraction of the outgoing radio waves.

Several features helped make radar an excellent visual aid for television weather. Displays were updated every few minutes, so viewers could see weather as it was unfolding. Radar's coverage area, on the order of a hundred miles in radius, corresponded well with the typical viewing area of a television station. Different types of precipitation — such as squall lines, isolated thunderstorms, and large areas of steady rain — were all easy to distinguish on radar; no involved explanations were needed from the weathercaster. Radar quickly became a standard tool in those Midwest and plains states often battered by severe weather. Instead of simply telling viewers that a severe storm was imminent, weathercasters could now show the storm's development as it occurred, giving credence to the warning.

Despite radar's obvious strengths, some features of a radar display made for public confusion. For example, outgoing radar signals travel at a very slight angle above the horizon. The beam gains elevation as it travels outward, because of the radar's orientation and the earth's curvature. This means that at large distances, the radar signal may completely overshoot the tops of clouds producing rain or snow. One can imagine a viewer's puzzlement upon seeing a crystal-clear radar display for her area as raindrops beat against the window! Ground clutter is another problem: Tall structures near the outgoing signal can reflect the beam as a storm might, creating a jumble of returns at the center of the radar image. The more skilled weathercasters made efforts to explain such quirks of the radar screen. Still, misinterpretations of radar are common in television weather. (One frequent error is to point out "stationary rainshowers" that are actually echoes from nearby mountaintops.)

By 1968, the maps of Lexington, Kentucky, weathercaster Frank Faulconer at WKYT included arrows and "clouds" that reflected polarized light to give an illusion of motion. (Courtesy Frank Faulconer)

A RETURN TO SCIENCE

Change of all sorts may have swept the United States in the 1960s, but
television-weather presentations hardly budged an inch visually. Even at
the decade's close, weathercasts were still using hand-prepared maps in virtually all markets. Progress that did occur in television weather during
the 1960s was largely due to a steady increase in professional standards.
The American Meteorological Society's seal-of-approval program certified
weathercasters in a handful of markets nationwide. Many weathercasters
were beginning to trust their audiences with a more intelligent delivery than
in the frivolous 1950s.

One example of the more scientific weathercast was the use of *isobars*.
These lines connect points of equal atmospheric pressure, circling around
high- and low-pressure centers. Narrowly spaced isobars are associated
with high wind, so the use of isobars on maps showed viewers at a glance
where conditions were calm, breezy, or turbulent. Of course, any weathercaster could simply slap isobars on a map, using National Weather Service
data. But explaining isobars' importance demanded a bit more sophistication than had been common in earlier weathercasting.

One major addition to weathercasts made its debut in the 1960s.
America's first weather satellite, TIROS I, went into space on April 1, 1960.
Only hours after entering space, TIROS began taking and transmitting

photos of cloud cover from 450 miles up.[3] The snapshots proved to be a gold mine for meteorologists, providing clear evidence of weather features that had been theorized for decades. Most notably, hurricanes could now be reliably spotted and tracked, even hundreds of miles from shore. Miami's National Hurricane Center quickly became the prime user of satellite images for weather forecasting. (Even into the late 1980s, satellites remained the most valuable tool for tracking hurricanes.)

Two Florida stations became pioneers in using satellite imagery on television during the mid-1960s. At Jacksonville's WJXT, meteorologist George Winterling pieced together small satellite shots transmitted via Weather Bureau facsimile into a larger picture suitable for broadcast each day.[4] Roy Leep, at Tampa's WTVT, went even further, installing equipment for direct satellite reception and then consolidating those pictures. The cut-and-paste method was needed because each of these early pictures was taken from a different vantage point in orbit.[5] While the end result was something of a patchwork, the sheer novelty of seeing the weather from space must have been impressive. Another pioneer in satellite-image use was Frank Field, of New York's WNBC, taking advantage of the Weather Bureau's proximity (in the same building as WNBC) to feature the first satellite shots televised in the Northeast.[6]

"Moving weather" was the often-used name of another weathercast technique that slowly gained popularity in the 1960s. The process was a crude form of animation using traditional forecast weather maps. Before each weather program, a series of still photos was taken of a standard hand-drawn or magnetic map. Between these shots, the weathercaster made small incremental changes in the position of fronts and other map features, moving them to their predicted locations. The final sequence of photos could then be run through very quickly to give the appearance of highs, lows, and fronts scooting across the nation. Sometimes very effective, this technique was only as good as its execution. Haphazard placement of the map features led to an uneven product, with fronts speeding up and slowing down at random.

Jacksonville's George Winterling was an early practitioner of moving weather, first using the process in 1965 to illustrate the approach of Hurricane Betsy. Winterling extended the idea to satellite pictures later in the decade, becoming the first weathercaster to show satellite loops on the air.[7] In 1984, Winterling received a special AMS award for "pioneering achievements in TV weather animation."[8]

Weather sets continued to evolve through the decade. Sliding panels and rotating map spools became common means of transcending the one- or two-camera limitation to show several maps in a single weathercast. Still, by 1969, weathercast technology had only inched forward from its level of 20 years earlier. The biggest changes were yet to come.

THE 1970s PROGRESS PICKS UP

If the 1960s was a fairly quiescent period for television-weather displays, the 1970s ushered in an era of technological innovation that accelerated into the next decade. Computers became inexpensive enough to make their way into the newsroom in varied applications. At the end of the 1970s, weathercasts were decidedly more colorful and visually pleasing than ten years before. Color television was no small factor in this transformation: by the late 1970s, a majority of American homes had color television, and nearly all network and local shows had abandoned black-and-white transmission.

Getting the Word Onscreen

One early and important outgrowth of electronics in the weathercast was the invention of character generators for the display of textual information. This device allowed a user to enter words and numbers into a computer and to superimpose the text on a background display of the user's choice. One of the first models, ANCHOR (Alpha-Numeric Character Generator), reached networks and a few local stations in the late 1960s. ANCHOR had its problems, though: Spacing between letters was constant, as on a typewriter. Thus, the letter *i* seemed to have extra space around it, while *m* appeared crowded. This aesthetic flaw was corrected in a subsequent character generator, the Ripley, that featured proportional spacing and width variations for each letter.[9] By the late 1970s, a host of companies were producing character generators, and the products were becoming standards in large and midsize television markets alike.

Weather was not the only news segment to benefit from character generators. Sportscasts were improved with the electronic posting of game results that once were handwritten. Captions were easily placed on news film, and crawls for news and weather were far simpler to create than before. Weathercasts used character-generated copy to display forecasts, current conditions, and statistics. Many stations overlaid weather data on a video background of local scenic spots, cloud features, and so on; the backdrop could be changed each day for added variety.

Satellite pictures became an integral part of local news during the latter 1970s with GOES (Geostationary Operational Environmental Satellites). For 15 years, the United States had launched several series of weather satellites that orbited Earth, taking pictures along the way. This constant motion made for large time gaps between pictures of a certain area on the globe, such as the United States. In 1975, GOES-1 became the first United States weather satellite to stay in position over the country, sending a picture every hour from the same vantage point.[10] Cloud features could now be closely monitored without data gaps. A day's set of photos could be

Roy Leep (right) was a pioneer in the use of satellite photos for television weather. Geostationary-satellite images came to WTVT, Tampa, beginning in 1975. (Courtesy WTVT)

assembled into dramatic satellite loops without the patchwork quality of earlier attempts.

GOES pictures made it to local weathercasts in the 1970s by several means. Each of the three major networks received daily satellite loops from the National Oceanic and Atmospheric Administration (NOAA). These, in turn, could be picked up by affiliates and used on local television. NOAA's standard facsimile lines also sent periodic satellite shots, albeit of poor quality for television use. A more expensive and exclusive method was to contract with private weather services for direct satellite transmission of pictures. One such system, Laserfax, made its debut on Tampa's WTVT in 1975. By the late 1970s, most large-market stations had incorporated satellite pictures into their weather segments. Smaller stations lagged behind because of the expense of satellite delivery or their lack of network affiliation.

As with radar, the appeal of satellites to viewers was obvious. People could see weather occurring across the entire United States at once. Moreover, satellite images topped radar displays in that they showed nearly *all* clouds, not just those dropping rain or snow.

Satellite loops brought even more realism to weather graphics, along with the ability to show how day-to-day weather evolves. For instance, the explosive growth of thunderstorms, with their bright images and rapid motion, could easily be contrasted with less dramatic cloud formations (such as stratus or cirrus) hovering elsewhere over the United States.

Showing the Storms

Radar's use in weathercasting took several steps forward in the 1970s. The most important was the introduction of "rainbow radar," a colorized version of the standard radar display. From its beginning, radar had been able to distinguish between areas of light and heavy precipitation by the brightness of its signal. On the early black-and-white radar screen, this distinction emerged in analog fashion: a strong storm would appear brightest white in the center, with the intensity gradually lessening toward the edges and the signal fading to grey.

By the mid-1970s, the computer technique known as analog-to-digital conversion enabled these signals to be transformed into five or six discrete levels of storm intensity. The same storm cell could now be displayed as a set of five or six concentric rings, each denoting a different rainfall rate. Areas between each ring were assigned colors according to intensity; red commonly denoted the heaviest rain; yellow, moderate intensity; and blue or green, lightest rainfall. Rainbow radar provided little more information in the scientific sense than traditional black-and-white displays. However, the concept did add interest to radar's appearance and became something of a fad among large-market stations in the late 1970s.

By the end of the decade, many large and midsize stations had their own radar transmitter-receivers, especially across the eastern two-thirds of the United States where severe weather was a frequent threat. These units varied greatly in quality, running the gamut from World War II–era discards to state-of-the-art models. Those stations unable or unwilling to purchase their own radar systems in the 1970s had another option: "dial-up" radar from the National Weather Service. A special facsimile-reproduction device could be attached to a phone line, so that stations could call NWS radar sites and receive a copy of their latest radar display. The quality of these images was not much better than that of a mimeographed photo, but dial-ups gave smaller stations the ability to feature radar reports from anywhere in the United States. Introduced in the late 1960s, dial-up radar grew slowly during the 1970s.

Clearly, weathercasts were looking different by 1979. The pace of change was picking up; electronic lettering, color radar, and satellite photos had all come to local news. Still, few stations or weathercasters were fully prepared for the revolution that was soon to transform weather graphics.

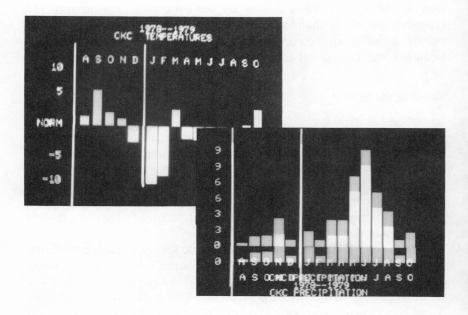

These charts, showing temperature and precipitation for Oklahoma City, appeared on KTVY in late 1979. Created on an Apple computer, they were among the first electronic graphics used in television weather. (Courtesy KTVY)

THE 1980s: COMPUTERS HIT WEATHERCASTING

In the late 1970s, a well-publicized burst of innovation in computer technology swept the United States and the world. Hand-held calculators dropped in price from hundreds of dollars to $10 or $20 as miniaturized circuits became commonplace. Digital watches and VDT screens spread across the country. By 1980, the computer revolution was poised to enter television news, and the lowly weather map was among the first elements of a weathercast to become transformed via computer. This metamorphosis was led not by the National Weather Service but by ambitious and innovative private meteorologists.

As personal computers such as the Apple came within reach of television-station budgets, companies set to work devising software for use on newscasts. The Quantel Paintbrush was one such package used in the creation of television art suitable for newscasts. Weather segments posed a larger challenge, though. Drawing a weather map was a mixture of art and science; factual material had to be worked into a pleasing format. How could a computer-graphics package be instructed to handle the mountains of data that go into a typical weather map? Private meteorologists and computer programmers began to collaborate on this problem. The result was a complex overlapping network of public and private services designed to tackle all aspects of computerized weather.

Programming the Weather

The first job was to convert weather data from the National Weather Service (NWS) into a form suitable for use in personal computers. Politics helped push this role upon private meteorological services. Until 1981, the NWS was both provider and channeler of weather details for the vast majority of weathercasts. Through contracted facsimile and teletype networks, the Weather Service sent its collected observations and computer forecasts to the mass media and to private weather firms. The latter, in turn, used NWS observations to make their own predictions.

After the election of President Ronald Reagan in 1980 came a massive push for the "privatization" of government activities, including weather-data dissemination. In earlier times, the National Weather Service might have helped create computer-graphics systems suitable for television. Under this political climate, such a role was discouraged; in fact, even the established NWS process of taking observations was challenged. As it happened, the quickly evolving world of computer technology made private companies more able to adapt NWS information for computers than the more slowly moving United States government might have been.

The other major task of these companies was to write the actual programs that would use Weather Service data to create full-color weather maps. As noted above, the real challenge was to pare down vast quantities of information into an attractive, uncluttered, yet informative display. Such a job was ideally suited for companies with experts in both computers and meteorology. A third necessity was to create hardware needed to absorb and display these computer graphics, as the Quantel Paintbrush was doing for nonweather graphics. While a standard personal computer could sometimes do the trick, stations going that route needed trained personnel to orient the setup for weather graphics.

Emerging as a leader in all three elements of computer weather was ColorGraphics Systems, Inc., a Madison, Wisconsin, company founded by Dr. Richard Daly (a University of Wisconsin scientist) and Terry Kelly (a Madison weathercaster). The two came up with Liveline I, a hardware system unveiled in 1981. Liveline was a tool for displaying weather maps on a preprogrammed set of geographic backdrops. It was an immediate hit, and succeeding Liveline units have made their mark on over 300 newsrooms, including most of those in the nation's large and midsize cities.

Of course, computer-friendly maps and data were also needed to make Liveline useful. A ColorGraphics subsidiary called Weather Central was created to complement the Liveline hardware. Weather Central analyzes and prepares forecasts from NWS data in a form ready for use with a Liveline or other graphics system. Stations may opt for both Liveline and Weather Central service or for only one of the two. If only raw data are needed (not forecasts), several other companies provide data in formats compatible with Liveline.

Accu-Weather, of State College, Pennsylvania, was another leader in 1980s weather graphics. Founded in the 1960s by meteorologist Dr. Joel Myers as a ski-forecasting service, Accu-Weather branched into more general forecasting for radio and television in the 1970s. For its radio clients, Accu-Weather provided short taped weathercasts tailored to a specific market and delivered by telephone (see Chapter 10). For television, the company provided its own interpretation of National Weather Service data. Before computer graphics became available in the 1980s, Accu-Weather maps were transmitted via facsimile or telecopier to its client television stations; the receiving weathercasters then had the task of manually enlarging the "faxed" map into a size and format suitable for television. In that era, the main benefit of Accu-Weather service over NWS facsimile and teletype was a product more tailored to a specific listening area than the generic Weather Service information.

The advent of computer weather graphics via Liveline-style hardware gave Accu-Weather and its competitors a stronger selling point. Weather maps could now be transferred directly from company headquarters to television-station hardware via modem (telephone hookup). Stations could thus be given a full array of customized maps ready for broadcast. Or, should a station want to design its own graphics, Accu-Weather could simply provide NWS data processed into a computer-ready format. Both Accu-Weather services, much like those provided by Weather Central, were founded in 1982 and had grown to several dozen television stations by the late 1980s.

Still another firm, WSI Corporation of Bedford, Massachusetts, provided data, graphics packages, and hardware, but not the forecasting resources of companies like Accu-Weather. (WSI broke off from Weather Services Corporation, its parent company, in 1983; the latter firm does extensive forecasting for radio and television.) To complicate matters further, WSI also sold computer graphics from Weather Central, for use with WSI arrangements of National Weather Service data. Such intermingled affairs make the world of weather graphics fascinating but confusing, especially for producers and weathercasters just becoming familiar with the field.

Weathercasts Go Uptown

During this period of rapid growth in weather graphics, private meteorological firms developed a number of innovative map displays. Three-
dimensional maps were introduced, showing the earth's curvature. Vivid
colors were splashed across the screen; for example, predicted high temperatures were depicted as bands of color ranging from dark blue or violet (at
the cold end of the spectrum) to crimson (depicting heat). However, one
often-overlooked disadvantage in using this explosion of hues was that
viewers with black-and-white sets found it hard to distinguish between the
resulting shades of grey.

The 1970s' rainbow radar was brought to a national scale in the 1980s
with the advent of nationally digitized color radar displays. These maps
combined reports from dozens of National Weather Service radars across
the country, then placed the result onto a United States background, retain-
ing the original maps' colored gradiations of storm intensity. The result was
a bright, attractive depiction of rain and snow patterns across the country.
By the close of the 1980s, private meteorological firms were working on
techniques to supplement the radar composite with ground reports of
precipitation, further adding to the complete national picture.

Chromakey: Sleight of Map

How did all these new graphics make it from the computer monitor to the
outgoing television signal? *Chromakey* was the secret, an ingenious system
allowing weathercasters actually to interact with computer-generated imagery. The chromakey process was invented by NBC in the 1950s* to merge
two filmed images into one picture. Its earliest application was in entertainment; for example, singer Tennessee Ernie Ford could be "chromakeyed"
onto a set of background singers performing in a separate location.[11] No
such electronic gadgetry was needed for television weather as long as hand-
produced maps were the norm. It was not until the early 1980s that the advent of computer graphics made chromakey essential for both news and
weather.

Weathercasting's use of chromakey begins with a base image of the
weather anchor and background set. The second, overlaid, image is the
computer-produced graphic (e.g., a weather map). To accomplish the
merging, the on-air person must stand before a large board of one solid
color, typically blue or green. The chromakey unit is electronically instructed to substitute all outgoing signals of that board's color with the

---

*NBC's original trade name for the technique was Chroma-Key. In subsequent years, that
name has become a standard term for the superposition devices made by various companies.

appropriate computer-stored graphic. So long as the weathercaster has no clothing of the chromakeyed color, she can move before the tinted backboard and appear to be moving in front of the superimposed weather map.

While pulling off this illusion, the weathercaster must also gaze at an off-camera television monitor showing the complete overlaid image and must coordinate her hand motions to "point at the map," a technique requiring no small skill. On top of this choreography, the weathercaster needs to keep up a running monologue that relates directly to the graphic being shown and the map areas being highlighted. Doing chromakeyed weather is thus a far more intricate process than simply sitting and reading news from a TelePrompter.

In using chromakey, it stands to reason that the backboard color cannot match the weathercaster's eyes or wardrobe. If it did, portions of the overlaid graphic would appear directly on the weathercaster. Such an inglorious fate has visited many; legend has it that CBS newscaster Walter Cronkite was once a victim of a chromakey mishap.

Doppler Makes Television

The impact of computer graphics overshadowed some other notable changes in television weather during the 1980s. One of these was the introduction of Doppler radar on weathercasts. Named for the scientist who discovered variations in sound frequency that depend on a listener's relative motion, Doppler radar goes conventional radar a step better by depicting wind speed as well as precipitation. Areas of high winds and their directions can easily be pinpointed on a Doppler, making it a valuable tool for detecting downbursts, tornadoes, and other dangerous weather phenomena.

Doppler use was confined to scientific research until early 1981 when Oklahoma City's KWTV and Minneapolis' KSTP became the first television stations to purchase and use Dopplers.[12] Over the next several years, stations in Dallas–Fort Worth, Wichita, Kansas City, and elsewhere installed Dopplers. By 1985, at least 26 stations had their own Doppler-radar units, including New York's WNBC.[13] Far more stations were using conventional radar, though. A 1985 survey found over half of all weathercasts featuring some type of colorized radar display.[14]

One reason for Doppler's relatively slow acceptance in television weather, aside from its hefty price tag of $1 million or more per unit, is its complicated display. In contrast to the clear definition of precipitation areas on standard radar, wind patterns on Doppler appear as a diffuse jumble of colors. The displays offer valuable information to people trained in Doppler interpretation but can easily mislead or confuse the average viewer (or weathercaster). Traditional radar, while unable to detect wind, needs much less explanation than Doppler.

Despite these problems, Doppler images are likely to show up on more and more weathercasts during the 1990s. Several government agencies will have deployed some 200 Doppler radars near airports and weather stations by 1995. Indications are that some television stations without Doppler will make arrangements to broadcast data from federal Dopplers as a public-service effort. Such a program was initiated in Oklahoma City during the spring of 1987 before the city's three major affiliates had their own Dopplers. The concept is in keeping with recent trends toward private dissemination of National Weather Service data. Still, the public's acceptance or rejection of the complex Doppler displays will ultimately determine whether this radar is to become a television-weather staple or an isolated curiosity.

Lightning is yet another storm element that found its way into television-weather graphics during the 1980s. Physicists invented a device in the 1970s that could pinpoint the location of a cloud-to-ground lightning strike within seconds of its touchdown. Antennae spaced some 100 miles apart detect the direction and strength of each flash; a central computer assembles these reports and figures the approximate location of each cloud-to-ground strike. Such a detection network, covering all or much of a state, can locate tens of thousands of lightning strikes during a single day of thunderstorms.

Noting the potential of their device for television-weather use, Lightning Location and Protection, Inc., of Tucson, Arizona, developed computer-graphic output displays suitable for television. In 1981, Atlanta's WXIA became the first United States television station to purchase its own lightning-detector network. The device has since been featured on weathercasts in several other large markets, including Denver and Minneapolis–St. Paul. Rather than purchase their own network, many stations have chosen to use data from government-owned detection systems that now blanket the United States. The ColorGraphics Liveline system features an interface to allow transmission of lightning-detector output supplied by outside agencies.

One major problem is the use of lightning displays on television in the brief time (only a few seconds) allotted for their use during a weathercast. Strikes are normally added to the display as they occur; however, a gap of one or two minutes between strikes would make for a static, less exciting display. The solution found by graphics specialists was to store five or ten minutes' worth of lightning data and to bring these strikes on the display during the weathercast, as though they were occurring instantaneously. Although potentially misleading, the technique does give viewers a quick summary of lightning progress over a fairly long time period. Even with this improvement, the graphic impact of showing lightning strikes remained understated, and a slowdown occurred in the systems' popularity during the latter 1980s.

The pace of innovation in television weather graphics showed little sign of dropping off as the 1980s came to a close. Government policy, the revamping of National Weather Service equipment, technical advances, and the increasing financial importance of local television news all pointed to the prospect of ever more colorful, sophisticated weather displays. In fact, the true challenge for weathercasters is separating the wheat from the chaff. So many types of weather-graphic displays are in the marketplace that stations must beware of purchasing a flashy set of maps that offer little real information. As always, the trained and intelligent weathercaster is the critical link in selecting quality displays and helping viewers interpret them.

6

Diversifying the Weathercast

Americans have long looked to the "weatherman" to keep them informed on the atmosphere's itinerary. In the first few years of television, the new medium gave people exactly what the word *weatherman* implies: a man, usually white, usually not too young or too old. Weathercasting thus reflected a society that shunted women and racial minorities as far from positions of authority as possible.

It quickly became clear in the 1950s that women could in fact be accepted as weathercasters — as long as the focus was kept on clothing, hairstyle, or anatomy. So began the brief ascendancy of "weathergirls" (a term that speaks volumes about the differences in status between these women and their male counterparts in weathercasting). By the early 1960s, the weathergirl craze had abated, and weather segments were once again dominated by white middle-aged men. Racial minorities were virtually absent from weathercasts, as they had been since television began.

This state of affairs changed radically in the 1970s, as civil-rights initiatives from the preceding decade started making their mark on television news. Black and other racial minorities finally gained spots on local weather programs. At the same time, the first large group of trained female weathercasters emerged from meteorology schools to begin correcting the negative stereotypes about women and weather created two decades before.

As the 1980s drew to a close, the ranks of weathercasters continued to diversify. Women now make up a significant portion of all weather anchors, holding down prime-time spots in cities as large as Philadelphia and on national cable networks. Racial minorities are less prominent in weathercasting in sheer numbers, with only a few dozen in local newscasts. However, some of the most highly prized jobs in television weather are held by minorities, including prime-time spots in New York and Los Angeles, and morning positions on all three major commercial networks.

WOMEN AND THE WEATHER

Women doing weather on television? The very idea was virtually unthinkable when television newscasting got under way in the late 1940s. During this formative period, women interested in nonentertainment television work were commonly relegated to positions closely tied to domestic life. One of the most prominent women on national news during the early 1950s was the former Miss America Betty Furness, who attained fame in commercials that extolled the virtues of home appliances.[1]

An even greater block to female weathercasters was society's ingrained suspicion of women's scientific abilities. Not even the most esteemed researchers were immune to the belief that women did not belong in meteorology or any other science. In 1949, Joanne Simpson became the first woman to earn a Ph.D. in meteorology. When she began her graduate work at the University of Chicago, one instructor told her that no woman would ever earn a doctorate in her field and that she need not waste her time trying.[2] (Simpson became president of the American Meteorological Society in 1989.)

As with many other trends, it was New York City that paved the way for the United States in accepting women as weathercasters. Carol Reed debuted on New York's WCBS in 1952; by all accounts, she was the country's first female weather reporter. The 26-year-old Reed was untrained in meteorology, but in this time of rapidly increasing competition between stations, WCBS seemed to count on the novelty of Reed's approach to bring success.

Reed did more than hold her own. She cultivated an energetic style that made her a local weathercasting favorite for 12 years. One of the most renowned features of a Reed weather segment was her traditional sign-off phrase, "Have a happy."[3] It proved to be one of those short, cheerful sayings perfect for television; its open-ended quality was especially appropriate for a truly mass medium.

With the rest of United States television searching for gimmicks in the mid-1950s, the idea of women weathercasters spread quickly. By 1955, just three years after Reed began, women made up a major fraction of all weather anchors, if not a majority. National press made much of the trend while popularizing the "weathergirl" tag. It was a significant choice of words. Somewhere between Carol Reed and the hundreds of protégées who followed, any notion of serious women delivering serious weather information had been lost.

Who were the women that rushed to fill television's newfound demand? Far more were entertainers than journalists or scientists. Among five female weather anchors spotlighted in a 1955 *TV Guide* article, Cindy Dahl (WTTG, Washington) was a "USO singer-dancer-comedienne"; Kay

Field (WISH, Indianapolis) was a "former name-band singer"; and Eugenia Burke (WARM, Scranton, Pa.) was "Miss Press Photographer." Exceptions did exist, though. Judy Marks (WOKY, Milwaukee) had "studied basic meteorology."[4]

Certainly, being from an entertainment background did not preclude women from doing competent weathercasts. Scattered around the country in the 1950s were women who, while not formally trained in meteorology, handled weather with the respect and clarity that some men with similar backgrounds did. Moreover, there was a tiny number of bona fide female meteorologists on the air. One of these was Marcia Yockey, who debuted in 1953 on WFIE in Evansville, Indiana, after ten years in the Weather Bureau. Yockey had planned to become a doctor, but World War II interrupted her college chemistry studies. She joined the bureau's Evansville office to replace forecasters who were called to military duty and brought that experience with her to television work.[5]

By and large, though, women weathercasters of the 1950s did their jobs without any training in meteorology. It was that lack of preparation, along with public skepticism of women's scientific skills and programmers' eagerness to trivialize the weathercast, that made "weathergirls" easy prey for critics. Many articles in both the popular press and scientific journals discussed the women-in-weather trend in a smug, flippant tone. These pieces seldom criticized a particular weathercaster; more often, they simply focused on the women's physical attributes and ignored their skill or lack of skill in conveying weather information. It was often presumed, even by scientists, that beauty precluded weathercasting ability. *Science News Letter* wrote in 1956: "Whether pretty girls or trained weathermen should present television weathercasts, long the subject of private discussion among weathermen, now is being openly debated."[6]

Crosses to Bear

Men's and women's weathercasts were equally gimmicky during this most gimmicky period of television. Puppets and cartoons were trotted out by both sexes. But women bore the special burden of having to play sex object, which sometimes entailed delivering the weather in various states of undress. Maxine Barrat (WITV, Hollywood, Fla.) did regular weathercasts clad in a bathing suit.[7] Ginger Stanley went Barrat one better on CBS's "Morning Show." For three weeks in 1956, Stanley gave weather reports while completely immersed in a huge tank of water. Stanley drew maps for her weathercast on the Plexiglas sides of the tub.[8]

Perhaps the greatest indignities of all were experienced by Tedi Thurman of NBC, whose weathercasts on the Jack Paar "Tonight" show of 1957 were just short of burlesque. Thurman appeared from behind a shower curtain each night to give a weather report laced with double entendres. Some examples, noted in a 1957 *TV Guide* profile: "Tomorrow will be kind of hot, with temperatures reaching over 100 in parts of Texas, Kansas, Missouri — and my apartment." "In the morning — rain. In the afternoon — dew. In the evening — don't." "Virginia will be very warm, and I'm just thrilled for poor Virginia." (Ironically, Thurman was a more experienced weathercaster than many of her television colleagues, having done radio weather for NBC News prior to "Tonight.")[9]

Even when the stars were fully clothed, appearance and fashion were still often considered the highlight of a woman's weathercast in the 1950s. Janet Tyler (WABC, New York) reported weather in the clothing appropriate for the next day. Thus, Tyler might be wearing coat and gloves, even on a warm prefrontal day.[10] In 1961, WABC Vice President Joseph Stamler told the *New York Times,* "We feel that women — or ladies — have greater acceptance than men [as weathercasters], because, well, with the combination of an attractive-looking personality the men prefer to look at and the women are attracted to because of the fashions they wear, we've really got a twofold program."[11]

Exit the "Weathergirls"

If anyone had thought the "weathergirl" era would ensure women a place in television news, their beliefs were quickly dashed. By the end of the 1950s, the trend in weathercasting was clearly away from women. *TV Guide* devoted a 1959 editorial to changes in television weather, commenting: "There are a few girls left around the country on weather-forecast shows, but these are either qualified forecasters or have long since learned to stick to the facts."[12]

Some markets lagged in the rejection of female weathercasters. New York City still had six women delivering weather in 1961, including two on WABC alone. In that year, the *New York Times* published a piece entitled "The Weather Girls Ride Out a Storm," noting the shift away from women doing weather and discussing New York City as an exception to the national rule.

What happened to the hundreds of women who had gained brief fame as weathercasters? Many of them left broadcasting for good, perhaps discouraged by their meteoric rise and fall. New York's Carol Reed was dismissed from WCBS in 1964 when that station dropped weather as a separate news segment.[13] When the station changed its mind and reinstated weathercasting less than two years later, Reed did not return.

Others who gave up weather shows by choice or by force stayed at television stations in the hopes of returning to on-air work. Lola Hall (KWTV, Oklahoma City) did weathercasting through much of the 1960s.

While not above using visual stunts on occasion, Marcia Yockey (WFIE and WTVW, Evansville, Ind.) grounded her weathercasts in solid meteorology. (Courtesy Marcia Yockey)

She left the airwaves as the station moved toward professional meteorologists, worked behind the scenes at KWTV for years, then returned as a news reporter in the 1980s.

Finally, there were those women who succeeded as longtime weathercasters by virtue of their knowledge, popularity, and sheer persistence. A prime example is Marcia Yockey, who continued doing television weather in Evansville from the mid-1950s until her retirement in 1988. Though Yockey enjoyed bringing humor to her shows on special occasions (one Fourth of July, she did her segment after flying onto the Ohio River with pontoons), she never abandoned serious meteorology. "I used isobars, fronts, and adiabatic lapse rates," Yockey recalls. "I gave [viewers] the map the way it should be."[14]

Once More, with Training

From the latter 1960s into the 1970s, the female presence in weathercasting was at a minimum. It took some time for the women's movement, which did not greatly affect mainstream United States culture until the early 1970s, to affect television weather. Moreover, the new awareness of sexism on television made programmers much more cautious about hiring unqualified female weathercasters. Before women could take advantage of this opportunity, they had to earn degrees, and until the 1970s, few women even considered embarking on a meteorology education. Slowly, though, more and more women found the courage to invade formerly all-male schools of meteorology. By 1981, some 10 percent of the nation's meteorology degrees were being awarded to women.[15]

One index of women's reemergence in television weather is the roster of American Meteorological Society seal-of-approval holders (see Appendix I). The first two women to earn AMS seals, June Bacon-Bercey and Virginia Bigler-Engler, were certified in rapid succession during 1972–1973. It was 1978 before a third woman received the AMS seal (Valarie Ann Jones), but five women earned seals in 1982–1983, and a similar pace continued through the 1980s.

Bacon-Bercey started her television career as a science reporter, unsure if doing weather would tarnish her credibility as a journalist. Despite her background in meteorology, "I did not want to do weather on television, only because at that time I felt it was still gimmickry for women, and I didn't want to prostitute my profession by being some kind of clown." On one afternoon in 1971, though, an unexpected absence of the regular weathercaster at Buffalo's WGR put Bacon-Bercey on the air as a substitute. She was an immediate hit, continuing for several years at the station.[16]

Even as qualified female weathercasters began making it on the airwaves, attitudes were slow to change. Kelly Lange began her television career doing weather for KNBC in Los Angeles. A 1973 *TV Guide* article on weathercasting began: "Blonde, deliciously pretty and size 8, Kelly Lange goes six months at a time on the air without being seen in the same outfit twice. Many of her followers, she claims, develop more suspense over what creation she will choose than they do over the smog readings in the Los Angeles basin."[17]

Still, progress was being made. Detroit's Marilyn Turner had begun weathercasting in 1958 when sexism was still rampant. In a 1975 *Parade* article, Turner described how she had objected to the "weathergirl" tag upon joining WXYZ in 1972. "I don't believe anyone over 21 should be called a girl," said Turner. "You don't call a man a weather boy."[18]

In the late 1970s and 1980s, women became significantly more visible as news reporters and anchors. Some of the women filling these spots had cut their teeth in television weathercasting, a point often neglected by media historians. Diane Sawyer, who became the first female regular on the CBS newsmagazine "60 Minutes," entered television as a weather anchor in her native Louisville. Marilyn Turner left weathercasting in the 1980s to become a Detroit talk-show host, and Kelly Lange became one of Los Angeles' star news anchors.

As a weathercaster for WGR (Buffalo) in 1972, June Bacon-Bercey broke new ground for both women and minorities. Bacon-Bercey was the first female recipient of an American Meteorological Society seal of approval. (Courtesy June Bacon-Bercey)

Going National

Inroads for women on network weather came more slowly than on local news. After the "weathergirl" era had passed, women were not seen doing weather on major-network television until April 1980 when CBS brought Valerie Voss onto its revamped news show "Morning." Voss was noteworthy in several respects: She was the first woman doing national weather in some 20 years, one of the first degreed meteorologists of either sex on a network news show, and a novice to broadcasting itself, having begun her on-air career in Milwaukee less than a year before. That inexperience made Voss' few months on CBS a trying time.[19]

"There was a lot of opportunity for me there if I had had experience," Voss says. "Three months into the job, CBS had me interview someone about Hurricane Allen. I had never interviewed anyone on television.... That was the beginning of my demise [at CBS]." Sessions with a vocal coach only increased Voss' insecurity. "I developed an actual stutter-type stumble on the air. I'd hyperventilate.... I was smart and articulate, so they thought that would translate into being a good broadcaster, even though I had no experience. Everyone after the fact said, 'Do you feel like Sally Quinn?'" (Quinn is the *Washington Post* reporter thrust onto a CBS morning program in 1973 with minimal training.) Voss was dismissed from "Morning," along with other cast members, in October 1980. She persevered, though, landing a spot in 1981 at New York's WABC doing weekend weather and weekday news reporting.[20]

Only one woman has followed Voss to major-network weathercasting in the 1980s: Linda Gialanella, who did weather for ABC's "World News This Morning," the early-news program preceding "Good Morning America," from 1982 until 1984. Joan Von Ahn was one of three weathercasters for public television's "A.M. Weather" in the late 1980s. Cable networks have also provided opportunity for weatherwomen to go national. Voss did weather at the short-lived Satellite News Network during 1982–1983. Since 1986 Voss has served as the morning weathercaster for the Cable News Network. In the late 1980s, CNN employed one other female weathercaster, Karen Maginnis.

Women are an integral part of The Weather Channel (TWC), television's largest single employer of weathercasters. From its inception, TWC has featured women in every element of on-camera programming. Weather anchor Liz Jarvis produced and anchored "When the Well Runs Dry," a one-hour special on water issues, in 1989. By that year, TWC included seven women among its 30 weathercasters.[21]

Local Progress and Problems

Recent advances in local news haven't been so dramatic, with the "weather-girl" era still in memory and programming executives resistant to change. Most television markets have at least one female weathercaster; usually, though, that woman holds a morning or weekend time spot. Such was the case for Nancy Russo at Washington's WJLA and Kristine Hanson on San Francisco's KGO. Rare is the large city that has a woman doing weather on the weekday evening news. Among the exceptions is Philadelphia, where Linda Gialanella is chief weathercaster at KYW.

While still in her twenties, Rebecca Reheis held a prime evening weathercasting position in the late 1980s at Salt Lake City's KTVX, whose viewing area spans much of the Rocky Mountain region. Reheis had already earned her AMS seal of approval, a rarity for weathercasters under 30. She started her television career in 1984 while finishing a degree in atmospheric science at the University of Kansas. That first weathercasting job gave her a sample of the blatant sexism that still existed at some stations.[22]

"Consultants started moving into the picture," Reheis recalls. "I thought that they [station management] were hiring me as a woman working toward a degree in meteorology. When I finally got my degree, they would not allow me to use the title 'meteorologist,' because that demeaned the weekday guy, who was not a meteorologist. Since I was a woman, that made it look even worse. They said, 'We'll give you business cards instead.' At that point, they started talking me into sweaters, opening up my neckline, and I knew that I was not hired as a meteorologist." After a brief period outside television weather, Reheis landed her Salt Lake City job in 1985.[23]

Reheis and Voss agree that society's expectations of women limit their freedom as weathercasters. Both find it hard to be rambunctious or comical on the air without risking their acceptance by viewers. "The problem with being a woman," says Reheis, "is that I can't do some of the fun things they [her competitors] do, simply because it would make me look like a silly woman. I have to be really cautious about what I do. . . . I've got blond hair, so that complicates everything."[24]

Voss notes that tokenism is an issue that persists for women in weather. The presence of a male-female news-anchor team may inhibit station managers from hiring a woman as weathercaster. "I think their feeling," Voss observes, "is that by having a female newscaster, they've supplied what they needed. They don't need to have another one, and in some ways a woman doing a number-one weather position can be a disadvantage. There'll be women who resent her, there'll be men who think she's stupid, and there are a lot of smart women who work in television weather who *do* come off looking stupid sometimes. It's not an easy thing to carry off."[25]

Age is another problem for women weathercasters. Due to society's emphasis on women as beauty objects and the late reemergence of women in television weather, there are many fewer middle-aged women than men in weathercasting. June Bacon-Bercey addressed the problem in a 1982 speech: "A woman earning an advanced degree in meteorology wants a career, not a trial balloon that will burst when she begins to push forty."[26] Or, as Valerie Voss puts it, "Who's going to want a forty-year-old weathergirl?"[27]

MINORITY WEATHERCASTING

For all the challenges women weathercasters have faced, they at least have a 40-year tradition of being on camera. Blacks, Hispanics, and members of other racial minorities have a much shorter history in weathercasting. Prior to the late 1960s, when civil-rights momentum began to shift from public accommodations to hiring practices, blacks were effectively banned from television weather (as well as news and sports). Hispanics' presence in weathercasting was limited to a few stations near the Mexican border.

Blacks in Weather: Few but Famous

The overwhelming whiteness of television weather was gently satirized by creators of a landmark series set in a television newsroom. Among the original 1970 ensemble of "The Mary Tyler Moore Show" was John Amos, the only black cast member, as WJM weatherman Gordy. Amos' character was among the first fictional portrayals of a weathercaster; it also ranks among the first inclusions of blacks in a situation comedy. Both these achievements were diluted by Gordy's small role in the show, as the character appeared in only a handful of episodes and then for only seconds. Still, the vast popularity of "Mary Tyler Moore" may have speeded accep-tance of minority weathercasters by providing a role model, however fictional.

Real progress came later in the 1970s, as the first wave of minority hir-ing reached television newsrooms. A few stations chose to advance two affirmative-action goals at once by recruiting black women as weather-casters. Chicago and Buffalo were among the first cities with black females doing weather. In Buffalo, June Bacon-Bercey carried unquestioned cre-dentials. She earned her meteorology degree at the University of Califor-nia, Los Angeles and had worked for years in the Weather Bureau and for the Atomic Energy Commission before gravitating to television.[28]

One of the deans of black weathercasters is Jim Tilmon. While many Chicago weather anchors hop between stations year to year, Tilmon has re-mained at WMAQ since 1970. Though not a meteorologist, he picked up weather knowledge as a copilot with American Airlines. Tilmon downplays the effect of being black on his acceptance among viewers: "I think people are much more interested in whether or not it's going to rain tomorrow."[29]

Other northeastern cities also proved hospitable markets for blacks in-terested in weathercasting. In 1977, Steve Baskerville took on weather duties at KYW in Philadelphia while also cohosting a talk show and hosting a daily children's program. New York City's first minority weathercasters were Don Sorreals, who joined WNBC in the late 1970s and later went to Washington's WRC, and Spencer Christian, doing weather on WABC in 1977–1981 and on ABC's "Good Morning America" in the later 1980s.

By the end of the 1970s, Hispanics also were making their mark on big-city weathercasting. Roberto Tirado was hired at New York's WPIX, and in 1978 Maclovio Perez found himself tapped for a weekend spot at Los Angeles' KCBS after four years of popularity as San Antonio's first full-time Hispanic weathercaster. "It was proof positive that an ethnic person can be on the air and accepted by the community at large," Perez recalls. "I wasn't just successful in the Hispanic market [in San Antonio], I was suc-cessful in the entire market."[30]

Progress for minorities at local stations continued into the 1980s, though the Reagan administration's decreased emphasis on affirmative ac-tion may have slowed the increase in numbers. The most visible break-throughs of the 1980s came in nationally broadcast weather on the major networks and on cable. In fact, minorities made up a majority of weather-

Steve Baskerville (WBBM, Chicago) became the first black weathercaster on a major network with the "CBS Morning News." (Courtesy WBBM/Ileen Ehrlich)

casters hired for morning-show slots in the decade's latter half. That trend got under way when CBS hired Steve Baskerville in January 1984. Following later in the decade were Spencer Christian on ABC's "Good Morning America," Mark McEwen (succeeding Baskerville on CBS), and Al Roker on NBC's "Sunday Today."

Roker's network position was actually a supplement to his weekday duties as chief weathercaster on WNBC in New York. For someone doing prime-time weather in America's largest city, Roker exuded modesty: "I'm just a guy you could see on the subway," he told an interviewer in 1985.[31]

Maclovio Perez closed out the 1980s as lead weathercaster in the country's second-largest television market. He found that Los Angeles audiences were quick to accept him as a person and not a token:

> It was another case in point where ethnic minorities can be accepted by the community at large. I wasn't known as the Mexican guy who did weather, I was known as Maclovio the weather guy. There was no differentiation, and that was exactly what I wanted.[32]

June Bacon-Bercey left television weather in the 1970s for a public-affairs post with the National Oceanic and Atmospheric Administration, but she looks back with fondness on her work in breaking television barriers:

I love challenges. Being a black woman, younger than my peers, everything
I did I had to excel in, just to be on an even level. And I didn't resent that.
I loved it.[33]

THE DISABLED

Unlike women and racial minorities, who made quick progress in television
weather once doors were opened, disabled persons found vast difficulties
in any kind of television work, including weathercasting. One expectation
of most people appearing on television is that they be energetic and able-
bodied. Even if someone bound to a wheelchair was both a good communicator and a meteorologist, his lack of mobility would make it difficult
for him to employ the animated gestures so commonly linked with television weather.

Still, there have been a few exceptional people who have managed
weathercasting in spite of handicaps. Viewers in Portland, Oregon, have
been watching one weather anchor for over 30 years; he has struggled with
incapacitating illness for more than half that period.

Jack Capell: Hanging In

. . . for promoting meteorology through the media of radio and television
in an educational manner, while serving as a shining example of tenacity,
perseverance, dedication, and enthusiasm to area listeners and viewers.[34]

So reads the statement announcing that Jack Capell would receive the
American Meteorological Society's 1989 Award for Outstanding Service by
a Broadcast Meteorologist. Though it certainly describes Capell in a
positive light, the statement only hints at the true magnitude of his
achievement.

Capell has been doing weather for Portland's KGW since 1956. In the
1960s, he conducted groundbreaking research on Pacific Northwest weather
while becoming a fixture on Portland television. But in late 1971, Capell was
diagnosed with amyotrophic lateral sclerosis (also known as Lou Gehrig's
disease). He was told by doctors to expect only a few years to live. Despite
the prognosis and steadily increasing disability, Capell continued doing
television weather on a reduced schedule through the 1970s and 1980s. Even
such handicaps as confinement to a wheelchair and loss of arm motion have
failed to prevent Capell from weathercasting.

Capell accommodates his limited mobility with a format much like
that of the early "Today" show weather segments: "I don't appear in front
of the weather map." Instead, he begins at the regular news set, going off

Jack Capell of Portland's KGW—an exceptional weathercaster. (Courtesy KGW)

camera as the maps are displayed. "The shots of graphics are all full screen," Capell notes. "Then, after the graphics are through, they come back to me full screen, and we wind up."[35]

An important factor in Capell's longevity has been the understanding of KGW personnel. "One general manager in the early 1970s questioned whether I should be continued," Capell says. There was "almost a revolt" in Capell's defense, he recalls. Since then, "the management has been very good in accommodating my handicapped situation. I give them a lot of credit."[36]

Assistance from my family has also been crucial. Capell's wife, Sylvia, joined him at KGW and helped him prepare each weathercast, working with maps and data. That job went to Capell's son in 1986 after Sylvia Capell suffered a stroke.[37]

After doing regular noon weathercasts into the early 1980s, Capell went to weekends, doing the 5:00 PM segments on Saturdays and Sundays. In that forum, he continues a serious approach to weather. Capell was the 19th person nationwide, and the first in Oregon, to earn the AMS seal of approval. "He displays both surface and upper air maps, as a real forecaster should,"[38] notes Bob Lynott, who once went head-to-head with Capell in Portland weathercasting. Jack and Sylvia Capell, says Lynott, "deserve honor beyond my limited ability to bestow."[39]

In the words of Jim Little, another KGW weathercaster, "Jack is an inspiration, not just to television weather people, but to everyone."[40]

7

Across the Nation

After 20 long years in the shadow of news and sports, nationally broadcast weather made a notable comeback in the 1980s. Local stations had taken on most weather coverage from the heyday of live television onward. But beginning in the late 1970s, a variety of distinctive national weathercasts hit the airwaves. From the joviality of NBC's Willard Scott to the sober, more technical approach of "A.M. Weather" on PBS, viewers could now take a look at the country's weather from several widely different perspectives.

Why the increase in national weather programming? One might think the average person would care little about weather in distant parts of the United States. However, America is a nation of ever-increasing mobility. More and more people hold attachments to several dispersed regions where they once lived or where loved ones now live. Perhaps following the weather at these spots helps people retain connections to distant places.

A more pragmatic reason for increased national weather coverage is transportation. Greater mobility means greater traveling, for both business and pleasure. Keeping up on conditions at a destination can help travelers avoid unpleasant surprises (as when shirtsleeves are packed for a spring trip to West Texas, and a snowstorm hits).

These changes in the American lifestyle might not have triggered such a boom in national weathercasts had there not been a proliferation of channels on which to air such programs. Cable television's sudden growth created enough airspace to be filled with all types of programming, weather included. The resulting shows culminated in what might be considered the ultimate weathercast: a 24-hour cable programming service (The Weather Channel) devoted entirely to workings of the atmosphere.

THE MAJOR MORNING PROGRAMS

NBC: "Today"

A true American institution, NBC's morning "Today" program has offered dependable weather coverage from its founding in 1952 through the 1980s. Personnel and styles have come and gone, but the sheer longevity of "Today" has engendered widespread trust in the show's weather information.

"Today" began as a largely spontaneous, lighthearted program. But by the end of the 1950s, "Today" was beginning to drop its more frivolous elements (such as the chimpanzee cohost J. Fred Muggs) in favor of a more serious approach. Evidence of this trend was the gradual shifting of weather coverage, at first assigned to host Dave Garroway and phone-in weathercaster Jim Fidler (see Chapter 3), to the program's news department. From the late 1950s until 1974, weather was handled by another original cast member, Frank Blair.

Blair, already a radio veteran when he joined "Today," gave weather the same no-nonsense treatment as any other news item. National maps were displayed, but Blair didn't stand and refer to them in usual weathercaster fashion. Instead, the maps simply filled the screen while Blair supplied off-camera narration from his anchor desk. "Today" was structured in half-hour blocks, so that a one- to two-minute weather update came after five to ten minutes of news from Blair at the beginning of each half hour.

One trend-setting element in "Today" weather reports was their promotion of the National Weather Service "Skywarn" program during the early 1970s. Skywarn was created as a daily guide to severe-weather potential across the United States. Each morning, the National Severe Storms Forecast Center in Kansas City, Missouri, issued a Skywarn statement outlining parts of the country predicted to have severe thunderstorms. The risk of severe storms for each area was conveyed by adjectives such as *isolated, a few, scattered,* or *numerous,* in ascending order of threat.

"Today" regularly broadcast Skywarn outlook areas, often alerting viewers well before severe weather materialized. The impact of this early warning cannot be precisely measured. However, some of the 1970s' fiercest severe-weather outbreaks were amply predicted by Skywarn. On the morning of April 3, 1974, "Today" viewers awoke to find a large part of the eastern United States slated to experience "numerous" severe thunderstorms. Later that day, over 140 tornadoes ripped through the Skywarn area in the largest one-day outbreak of twisters ever recorded. Thousands of people were injured and over 300 people died.[1] The airing of Skywarn forecasts on "Today" may well have prevented even greater death and injury by creating early awareness of the threat.

After Frank Blair's retirement in March 1975, anchor Lew Wood took over news and weather duties for "Today," keeping Blair's format. However, the program's sit-down weathercast was nearing its end. ABC countered in 1976 with "Good Morning America" (GMA), complete with morning television's first on-camera weathercaster, John Coleman. Perhaps in response to the success of that show, "Today" followed suit and hired Bob Ryan as its first on-air meteorologist in 1978. Ryan's acknowledged expertise didn't halt the downward slide in popularity of "Today." By early 1980, GMA surpassed "Today" in ratings for the first time.[2]

The Willard Era

Back at the drawing board, "Today" tried again, this time hiring a Washington weathercaster of limited meteorological background but great enthusiasm. Their choice, Willard Scott, made his debut on March 10, 1980. By the end of that year, Scott was on his way to becoming the most well known weathercaster in television history.

Scott's career began at Washington's WRC radio (see Chapter 3). In 1967, Scott filled in for WRC-TV's evening weathercaster; the job proved ideal for Scott, and his filling-in lasted 13 years. While at WRC, Scott honed a weathercasting style of exuberant antics mixed with a concern for small-town America. He made little effort to homogenize that distinctive approach upon joining "Today," leading some critics to brand him insincere. Gerry Davis writes in her *Today Show:*

> Was he using his hash browns, moonshine, love thy neighbor, hearty ha-ha, and good-ole-boy talk as just an act, or did he really mean what he said? ... Initially, complaints did come in, but before long people realized that Willard was for real—he wasn't acting.[3]

Scott's popularity on "Today" quickly reached levels unmatched by a morning personality since the 1950s as he received thousands of fan letters each week.[4] After several more years, "Today" was once again the highest-rated network morning program.

Willard Scott is perhaps the preeminent example of humorist as weathercaster. He has no formal meteorological background and readily admits that delivering weather news is secondary to his role as entertainer and goodwill ambassador. Of his WRC weather segments, Scott has been quoted repeatedly as saying, "A trained gorilla could do this job every night."[5] Scott's "Today" weathercasts, true to that attitude, lend themselves to a deemphasis of weather. Following each news report, Scott delivers one to two minutes of nonweather patter before going on to a very traditional weather map prepared by an off-camera meteorologist. ("Today" failed to join the computer-graphics bandwagon in the 1980s, resolutely sticking to a single artist-rendered map, although a computerized "highlight of the day" map was added in the mid-1980s.) Actual weather discussion comprises only a minute or so of Scott's delivery.

To his credit, Scott is meticulous about mentioning areas with threatening or extreme weather, even to the point of noting specific severe-weather watches in effect. One meteorologist-weathercaster in a midsize city praises Scott's map discussions as informative in spite of being laced with humor. Still, the highly successful "Today" weathercast of the 1980s will likely be remembered far more for the ebullience and warmth of its host than for the completeness of its information.

ABC: "Good Morning America"

"Happy news" became the dominant trend across the country's locally originated newscasts in the early 1970s. Interaction between anchors was stressed, in contrast to the rigidly segregated news, weather, and sports segments of the 1950s and 1960s. Producers strove to give the programs an aura of friendliness and affability. The tone was lighter and the pace quicker than before.

ABC's "Good Morning America" (GMA) brought these concepts into network news in 1976 to become the first serious competition for NBC's "Today." (An ABC show called "AM America" preceded GMA by one year but met with little success.) Very similar in structure to "Today," GMA featured male and female cohosts, a two-hour time slot divided into half-hour segments with news leading off each half hour, in classic "Today" fashion. But while "Today" maintained something of a hard-news orientation through the 1970s, GMA was developed primarily as entertainment and "information." Hosts David Hartman and Nancy Dussault, both from backgrounds in acting rather than journalism, greeted the audience from couches in a set resembling one vast suburban living room.[6]

Weather played a major role in this new morning program. In GMA's first year, newscaster Steve Bell read the weather in much the same fashion as Frank Blair and Lew Wood had been doing on "Today." But in 1977, John Coleman joined GMA. Coleman was a bona fide weathercaster with nearly two decades of experience in Omaha, Milwaukee, Chicago, and other Midwest markets. At Chicago's WLS, Coleman had become an integral part of that station's "happy news" by reviving the gimmicky-weatherman tradition of the 1950s. His on-screen antics at WLS included making doughnuts on a frigid winter night and delivering weather atop the 110-story Sears Tower during its construction. (He now defends that stuntsmanship as a way to draw viewers before giving them serious weather details: "We got a heck of a rating, then I cashed that rating in and built the best weather office in Chicago.")[7]

The humorous side of Coleman's delivery was toned down on national television. In fact, his GMA weathercasts were considerably more sedate than those of counterpart Willard Scott on "Today." Coleman hardly disdained humor on GMA, but he also included a fair amount of hard meteorology. A measure of Coleman's commitment to quality television weather was his role as founder of The Weather Channel.

"Good Morning America" was a network pioneer in weather graphics during its first several years. Coleman was the first on network television to use current satellite pictures, now a standard weathercasting element. GMA weather also instituted the novel combination of superimposing electronically drawn frontal boundaries on satellite pictures, enhancing the understanding of both maps. "I would tend to do a slow dissolve from one to the other, and show both elements full but also briefly superimposed over one another."[8] This creative use of weather illustration reflected ABC's status as the network most innovative with electronic graphics during the late 1970s and 1980s.

Coleman left his GMA post in 1983 to joined WCBS in New York. Replacing him was meteorologist Dave Murray, followed three years later by Spencer Christian, who finished out the decade on GMA.

CBS Morning Programs

Reviewers have long praised CBS for the quality of its news coverage. From the early 1950s, when an Edward R. Murrow documentary triggered the end of Senator Joseph McCarthy's anti–Communist crusade, many CBS news efforts have been popular and critical successes. Despite such triumphs, the network has struggled fruitlessly for decades to create a successful morning-news show. With each of the 26 changes in format from 1953 to 1988 came shifts in the way weather was presented. Much of that history is lost, though, since the quickly changing shows received little press attention.

Through the early 1960s, "weathergirls" reigned supreme on CBS morning-news shows. As that trend faded nationwide, CBS relegated its morning weather to news anchors, as "Today" had done on NBC. But by 1980, full-fledged weathercasters had been added on NBC and ABC morning programs. CBS countered by hiring the first female meteorologist to do network weather, Valerie Voss. One of the first women to earn the AMS seal of approval, Voss' manner on CBS was straightforward, contrasting with the antics of Willard Scott on NBC. She told a New York newspaper, "I don't want to be a stick-in-the-mud, but I need to be taken seriously. That's more important than anything else."[9]

Despite some positive reviews, Voss' tenure at CBS lasted only six months (see Chapter 6) before another format change arrived. Gordon

Barnes took on weathercast duties in late 1980, followed by Steve Deshler. In January 1984, Steve Baskerville joined the next CBS morning effort, becoming the first black weathercaster on network television. Baskerville's easygoing delivery kept him on CBS through a series of "CBS Morning News" cohosts and formats.

Baskerville and his colleagues were replaced in January 1987, as CBS tried a morning show styled after "Good Morning America." "The Morning Program" lasted only 11 months under critical fire. However, weathercaster Mark McEwen stayed on through the late 1980s. McEwen used his background in comedy and radio to deliver show-business and pop-music reports as well as weathercasts.

"A.M. WEATHER"

Viewers hungry for substantial weather information were given an alternative to the three commercial networks in October 1978 when the Public Broadcasting System unveiled "A.M. Weather." With a format that held remarkably constant over a decade, "A.M. Weather" earned a place as the most thorough and least flashy among nationally broadcast weather presentations.

"A.M. Weather" evolved from a weekly update for pilots, "Aviation Weather," produced at the Maryland Center for Public Broadcasting from 1972 to 1976. The first show had gradually earned a nationwide following, prompting the idea of a more frequent telecast. "Aviation Weather" was largely sponsored by the Federal Aviation Administration (FAA); FAA personnel anchored, and the National Weather Service provided brief taped voice-overs tailored to each local viewing area.[10] Preventing any further NWS involvement was a National Oceanic and Atmospheric Administration (NOAA) policy that forbade NWS employees from appearing regularly on television. This policy was written in the 1950s to keep commercial television stations or networks from gaining unfair advantage through the use of government resources (see Chapter 3). But in 1975, NOAA altered its position, allowing its employees to appear regularly on noncommercial television.[11] This opened the door for "A.M. Weather" to begin as a daily feature on some 130 public-television stations.

Two NOAA meteorologists, from a rotating staff of three, anchor the 15-minute show each weekday morning. Two live versions are produced each day and transmitted to Public Broadcasting System affiliates nationwide for immediate or delayed broadcast. Like "Aviation Weather," "A.M. Weather," is produced at the Maryland Center for Public Broadcasting in Owings Mills. Over a dozen aviation-related groups have sponsored "A.M. Weather," including the Aircraft Owners and Pilots Association, Phillips

Sharing the anchor duties in 1989 on "A.M. Weather" (PBS) were meteorologists Joan Von Ahn, Carl Weiss, and Wayne Winston. (Courtesy Maryland Public Broadcasting)

Petroleum, Beech Aircraft, and the Lawyer-Pilots Bar Association. Several major weather-graphics and forecasting companies have provided support in kind; these include Environmental Satellite Data, Inc., Weather Services Incorporated, Satellite Information Service Corporation, and KAVOURAS.[12]

With no advertising cutting into its quarter-hour time slot, "A.M. Weather" can delve into far more detail than the usual weathercast. Some 16 to 22 maps are taken directly from National Weather Service products and transferred by artists onto clear plastic overlay maps — a fairly low-tech approach compared to the electronic graphics on virtually all local weather shows by the late 1980s. With such a large selection of maps on hand, though, such features as upper wind speeds, agricultural data, or snow cover can be routinely displayed. The show's format follows the standard chronological sequence of current weather and forecast weather used on television since the late 1940s. As with the early "Today" show, the anchors stay seated off-camera during most of the program while maps fill the screen. The NOAA-supplied weathercasters stick closely to the forecasts and warnings issued by local Weather Service offices. Outlooks are thus more conservative and carefully worded than those from many local weathercasters.

Carried on some 300 PBS affiliates nationwide, "A.M. Weather" has become an audience favorite and a cult hit among pilots. The show has also been used in meteorology instruction at San Jose State University and other schools.[13] Even taking into account the 24-hour weather information now available on cable television, "A.M. Weather" has carved a distinct niche by providing some features unavailable elsewhere and packing that information into a brief no-frills format.

THE WEATHER CHANNEL

Few observers of television in the 1950s would have predicted the creation of an entire television channel devoted to live weather coverage. The Weather Channel (TWC)* proved many skeptics wrong by becoming a profitable operation after just three years of existence. TWC in the late 1980s was reaching some thirty-five million Americans with the kind of detail and resources early weathercasters could only dream of.

Laying the groundwork for TWC and its fellow cable networks was tremendous growth during the 1970s in the number of United States homes wired for cable. Isolated mountainous areas had relied on cable television for years, but only in the 1970s did the technology make inroads on large cities and then on the rest of the United States.[14] Cable News Network (CNN) began its nationwide 24-hour broadcasts in June 1980; it featured news reports similar to those on noncable networks, but offered more frequent and more in-depth coverage. With CNN's success at 24-hour informational programming, a precedent for The Weather Channel was established.

It was John Coleman, of "Good Morning America," who came up with the notion of a "weather channel." While pleased at the nationwide exposure of his GMA work, he was at the same time frustrated with its time constraints. One incident on June 30, 1978, made him wonder if struggling against the clock was worth it.

> I had the weather for Friday, Saturday, Sunday, and the [July Fourth] holiday to report, for all fifty states, and I had significant weather develop-

*The Weather Channel is a registered trademark of Landmark Communications.

ments—tropical storms, major cold front, big tornado outbreak in the works, unseasonable snow in the mountains, massive rainfalls, major drought underway in the West. I had an awful lot to talk about.

Seconds before I went on the air, the weathercast was shortened from two and a half minutes to a minute and a half, because they wanted a little more time for an interview with a Hollywood star coming up. It was done with total disregard for the weather situation.... I got off the air so frustrated, I really couldn't function.[15]

Recognizing cable television's growth and its potential for specialized programming, Coleman asked the Nielsen Co. to study public reaction to the idea of continuous television weather. He then took his concept and the positive survey results to Landmark Communications, a Virginia-based media company. Landmark agreed the idea was viable and named Coleman president and chairman of the newly formed network. After months of development and creation of a custom studio in Atlanta (chosen due to already-available satellite links and Coleman's desire to move south), The Weather Channel began broadcasts on May 2, 1982.[16]

The first years of TWC were marked by financial turbulence. Early losses were significant: by 1983, the network was reportedly at least $7 million in debt.[17] Differences in management philosophy led to Coleman's departure from TWC in 1983. In the next year, Landmark began charging cable companies a fee of five cents for every household receiving The Weather Channel.[18] That influx of revenue and an improving economy helped TWC become solvent by 1985 and a moneymaker in the late 80s.

Wall-to-Wall Weather

Developing content and format for TWC was a less imposing venture than arranging finances, though not without its pitfalls. The challenge of covering weather for an entire country without dwelling on any location had led to the short, superficial updates standard on network news. With the luxury of time and the help of technology, TWC managed to go against tradition to provide in-depth coverage on both national and local levels.

The core of The Weather Channel's programming falls well within the framework established by decades of earlier weathercasts. Most of the total on-air time consists of standard weather-anchor narration before a chrom-akey map display. Monotony is reduced through distinct packaging of weather detail into small chunks. Each hour of TWC programming is divided into 18 to 32 segments of one to three minutes each. These include extended-forecast discussions ("A Look Ahead"), nationwide satellite and radar views, and severe-weather outlooks (e.g., "Tropical Update" during hurricane season).

A number of TWC segments are expressly tailored to fit advertisers'

The largest single source of televised weather information in the 1980s was The Weather Channel, serving over 35 million cable viewers. Dozens of meteorologists worked behind the scenes (left) and on the air (right) to provide 24-hour weather. Local conditions are frequently displayed (see bottom right). (Courtesy The Weather Channel)

products. For example, hourly "driver's reports" are sponsored by the tire manufacturer Michelin. The company's logo is displayed prominently during the segment, and a Michelin commercial normally follows. In the huckster tradition of early television, some TWC weathercasters even do out-and-out plugs completely unrelated to weather. An "Eating Smart" feature is aimed purely at promoting food-sponsor products such as cheese and yogurt.

The most innovative feature of Weather Channel programming, and a big viewer draw, is the specialized local-forecast display. From eight to fourteen times each hour, viewers are shown a simple teletext screen with the forecast and conditions for their locality as provided by the National Weather Service. These reports for over 700 regions of the United States are assembled and distributed through TWC's Weather STAR, a satellite receiver that processes National Weather Service data from around the country and sends the appropriate information to hundreds of cable companies. The same device is used to transmit severe-weather information by breaking into normal TWC programming (only in the affected regions) and giving the details via teletext. Viewers of TWC thus receive much the same Weather Service information that viewers of local television would get.[19]

means of disseminating local severe-weather information; people watching these networks could be uninformed of even life-threatening severe weather.

Working at TWC

Automation may take care of local forecasts, but TWC still requires dozens of weathercasters to give national roundups. These anchors face a far greater workload than their local-station counterparts. While the latter typically appear on-screen only 20 minutes or so per workday, TWC talent spend at least 75 minutes a day before the cameras.[20] Even the youngest, most inexperienced broadcasters quickly gain poise and confidence with this routine. The continual nationwide exposure often leads to Weather Channel weathercasters being recruited by local stations for less strenuous spots. Still, almost half of the original TWC anchors have stayed on through the 1980s.[21]

As in local weathercasting, on-air talent at TWC vary greatly in background. Some two-thirds have meteorology degrees; others majored in communication or a similar field and picked up weather knowledge on the job. A few local weathercasters with decades of experience have joined TWC. However, most Weather Channel anchors are in their twenties or thirties, hoping the hard work and exposure will enhance their careers. Assisting TWC weathercasters is a background staff of some 40 meteorologists and ten computer-graphic artists who take National Weather Service information and tailor the data for TWC's many specialized segments.[22] The network's forecasts often differ from Weather Service outlooks, though NWS severe-weather warnings are broadcast without alteration.

Audience research at TWC reveals the significance of the network's local coverage. Most viewers tune in for a scant five or ten minutes at a time, with only the most devoted weather buffs watching over 30 minutes at once. Noting this pattern, TWC has emphasized quick viewing in its ad campaigns, encouraging people to switch to TWC between prime-time programs. Though few viewers watch for long periods, a sizable number do tune in frequently. By 1989, The Weather Channel was being offered on some 3,600 cable systems nationwide.[23]

With The Weather Channel firmly in place on the cable selector, viewers need never fear a dearth of national-weather programming. Other cable networks also devote varying periods of time to weather. The most notable of these is Cable News Network, with two to three one-minute updates per hour featuring a stand-up weathercaster and chromakeyed maps. Ironically, though, the very success of TWC may act against the development of major weathercasting efforts on other networks.

The good news for weather-conscious viewers is that television programmers now realize that a large audience is ready for complete, continuous national weather coverage. Though it took three decades to occur, that realization is likely to shape national telecasting for many years to come.

8

When Minutes Count

Imagine this scenario: A traveling salesman drives through Iowa on a muggy May afternoon. Storm clouds gather on the horizon. A stray raindrop hits the windshield.

Pulling into a small town, the salesman calls it a day and checks into a Main Street motel. Torrential rains descend as he hurries into his room, luggage in hand. Suddenly, the rain stops. A brief silence is broken by the ominous wail of a storm siren. What does the worried salesman do?

If he's like the majority of the United States public, he turns on the TV. Television is the overwhelming medium of choice for severe-weather information, especially in those tense moments just before a storm strikes. Radio has a long history of similar coverage, and it remains an important information source (especially, for instance, when a storm has knocked out electric power). But television reigns supreme as the electronic source of security in most severe-weather situations.

This public-service role is one of television's least appreciated functions. By transmitting National Weather Service warnings—which have themselves vastly improved during television's history—weathercasters have no doubt saved hundreds, even thousands, of lives. Rare is the television program that can affect people so directly.

Station managers haven't been blind to the power of severe-weather coverage. Many have learned that warnings can be a ratings booster as well as an aid to the public. And those weathercasters who choose to deviate from National Weather Service information often use storm coverage to highlight the independence of their forecasts.

WARNINGS BEFORE TELEVISION:
LET THE PUBLIC BEWARE

The evolution of severe-weather warnings occurred in tandem with the development of both meteorology and mass media. Before radio and television, the warnings themselves were often primitive. America's worst natural disaster to date amply illustrates the utter failure of weather alerts in the days before electronic media.

On the night of September 8, 1900, Galveston, Texas (the state's largest city at that time) was devastated by a hurricane that caught the populace almost totally unaware. Late on the afternoon of the eighth, as seas rose and the barometer dropped, Isaac Cline, of the Galveston Weather Bureau, tried to obtain authority for a hurricane warning from Weather Bureau headquarters in Washington. When all telegraph lines failed, Cline took a horse-drawn wagon down Galveston Island, warning beachgoers of the impending storm. The unapproved warning saved many lives, but 6,000 people died in the hurricane, including Cline's wife.[1]

The disastrous toll in Galveston reflected both a communications system prone to disruption and an overcentralized warning system within the Weather Bureau. Radio's debut in the 1920s helped solve the first problem. As early as October 1921, navy radio stations warned ships in the Caribbean of an approaching hurricane "of tremendous energy such as few vessels could outride or escape without loss or great damage." But, reported the *Bulletin of the American Meteorological Society,* "ships had been turned back by the warnings sent out and not a single one was lost or seriously damaged."[2] Despite the clear utility of radio in hurricane warnings, such alerts remained a low priority for the Weather Bureau. It took a record 21 tropical storms in 1933 to produce change. Two years later, hurricane-forecast centers were established in Jacksonville, Florida; New Orleans; and San Juan, Puerto Rico.[3]

This expanded network could not keep all storms from slipping through the cracks, though. On September 21, 1938, a powerful hurricane approaching the Carolinas veered north, a move which usually precedes a turn east to open waters. Weather Bureau officials in Washington gave the all-clear for the entire East Coast, and the message was promptly fed via radio to millions.[4]

Unbeknownst to government forecasters, the hurricane was about to be driven by a powerful upper-air steering current into Long Island and New England at over 60 MPH. Morning forecasts in New England newspapers and on radio had called for rain and breeziness; by evening, gusts at Blue Hill, Massachusetts, reached 186 MPH.[5] Hastily written warnings went out on radio only as the storm was raging full force, with veiled references to a tropical storm moving offshore.[6]

Mass media could have sounded the alarm in New England if warnings had been issued at the time. Historian William Manchester sums up public opinion of the era in calling the bureau a "slack outfit."[7] But if there was negligence, there was also a lack of knowledge. Ship reports that could have indicated the storm's northward turn were absent, and they were the only means of monitoring oceanic weather in this presatellite period.

Hurricanes didn't always take the United States by surprise in the 1930s. When the storms were detected early enough and sufficient warning was issued, radio played a crucial role in alerting people. Grady Norton became a Florida legend in the 1930s and 1940s as media liaison for the Jacksonville hurricane-forecast center. Several dozen radio stations along the Florida coast transmitted Norton's broadcasts during storm threats.[8] Robert Burpee described Norton's approach for the journal *Weather and Forecasting:*

> He had an Alabama drawl, spoke in a folksy way with a dry sense of humor and translated meteorological jargon into a language that everyone could understand.... When protective action was urged, he communicated a sense of urgency over radio or television that motivated people to respond to his warnings.[9]

Norton died while covering Hurricane Hazel in 1954, just as television was beginning to usurp his preferred communication channel.[10] His career stands as a prime example of the Weather Bureau's high-profile image during radio's reign of peak influence.

Twisters: Seen but Not Heard

In contrast to the increasing visibility of hurricane warnings during the 1930s, tornado alerts were nonexistent. The Weather Bureau's longtime policy had been to quash any belief that tornadoes could be predicted or even that people might be notified of an approaching twister.

Granted, knowledge of tornado behavior was sparse. While hundreds of these violent windstorms stuck the United States each year, most covered only a few miles and lasted just minutes. Trying to warn people of such fleeting events posed obvious problems. Still, there was some evidence that the general conditions leading to tornadoes could be forecast. Sergeant J. P. Finley, part of the original military-based National Weather Service, developed a system in 1884 for predicting tornadoes up to 16 hours in advance on the same broad scale as today's NWS tornado watches. Though Finley reportedly attained some success, none of his forecasts were made public, and his research ended in 1887 with agency wide cutbacks.[11]

From Finley's era through the Great Depression, the word *tornado* could not be used in any Weather Bureau public statements. Fear of panic and a distrust of rapidly improving communications systems seem to have dictated Bureau policy during these 50 years. The Tri-State Tornado is a case in point. This monstrous twister or series of twisters tore across Missouri, Illinois, and Indiana over several hours on March 18, 1925. Though the storm moved on an arrow-straight path, no coordinating agency tracked its progress, and thus no warnings made it on telegraph wires or radio. Nearly 700 people were killed.[12]

In 1938, the ban on mentioning tornadoes in Weather Bureau statements was lifted.[13] However, forecasters were still leery of frightening the public, and the status quo prevailed. "Severe local storms" remained the euphemism of choice in the bureau's public statements for another decade.

STORMS ON CAMERA: THE INFLUENCE OF TELEVISION

Though advances in meteorology had come at an increasing pace between World Wars I and II, the postwar era brought far greater progress. Such technical innovations as radar and upper-wind tracking made it possible to follow and predict storms with new precision. Television made its debut just as these tools were being incorporated into severe-weather-warning procedures. In some cases, television helped moved the process along.

Hurricanes: High Seas, High Ratings

By the time television began entering homes in the late 1940s, hurricane prediction was on the upswing. Upper-air observations from planes and weather balloons had become far more frequent, helping to locate the steering currents that control hurricane motion. Special reconnaissance flights into tropical storms, begun during World War II in the Pacific Ocean, brought precise data on the motion and intensity of storm centers. All this information gave early weathercasters more to talk about on television than had been available to their radio counterparts.

In the early 1950s, a period with few hurricanes, pioneer weathercasters had a chance to refine their hurricane-coverage techniques. Without such graphic aids as satellite pictures, there was little to show but handdrawn maps. Nevertheless, the pattern for hurricane coverage was established early. This included mention of distant storm threats on regular daily-weather segments; occasional updates on station breaks if a storm was a day or so away; and near-continuous coverage during hurricane warnings, with broadcasts running 24 hours a day until the threat passed.

Within this framework, there was considerable leeway for individual weathercasting styles. The clowning approach popular in the 1950s did not normally extend to hurricane coverage, but some stations clearly devoted more time and energy to tropical systems than others. A few coastal weathercasters gained regional fame for their frequent and informative discussions. One of these leaders was Nash Roberts, "Mr. Weather" of New Orleans. Roberts began weathercasting at WDSU in 1948 and became a television fixture in the 1950s during hurricane threats. His in-depth discussions and customized forecasts (which sometimes differed from Weather Bureau outlooks) were seen on various New Orleans stations through the 1980s.[14]

The progress of both hurricane forecasting and television weathercasting was tested in 1954 and 1955 when a string of intense storms pounded the United States eastern seaboard. Hurricane Carol brought 105-MPH winds and a near-record tide to Providence, Rhode Island, on August 31, 1954. Weathercaster Art Lake had to deal with Weather Bureau statements that lagged behind the storm itself.

> All we had in those days was what the Weather Bureau put out. They acknowledged that tides were running excessively high on the south coast of Rhode Island, near the mouth of Narragansett Bay. At the same time, we had about a foot of water in the streets of Providence, which is some forty miles to the north.[15]

Carol was only the first of five hurricanes to strike New England within a 12-month period, causing 154 deaths and over $1 billion in damage in that region alone.[16] The unprecedented string of storms caused the Weather Bureau to upgrade its dissemination of hurricane news to radio and television, reducing the sort of delays Art Lake noted. One help to the media was the bureau's new policy of naming tropical storms after women (and men, from 1979 on). The naming gave hurricanes more individuality and simplified their mention in weathercasts.

Though television proved helpful during the hurricanes of the 1950s, it was no insurance against major death tolls. In poor, rural areas, television sets were few and far between. Hurricane Audrey struck low-lying southwest Louisiana with unusual strength in 1957. Most of the isolated rural residents had access to only one radio station located well inland, whose advisories were tailored for the weaker, delayed effects expected there.[17] One announcer on that station reportedly misconstrued the term *hurricane's eye,* creating a false sense of security among listeners. Thousands near the coast failed to evacuate, and over 500 were killed.[18]

Audrey was one of the last major hurricane catastrophes. Satellite coverage of the Gulf of Mexico and Atlantic Ocean, beginning in the early 1960s, gave forecasters far more advance knowledge of hurricane development than ever before. At first, the National Hurricane Center had primary access to these pictures; it was not until the late 1970s that satellite shots of hurricanes became routine on local and national newscasts. However, some Florida weathercasters made earlier use of satellite shots. Roy Leep, of Tampa's WTVT, installed his own receiver for satellite signals in March 1966, making the pictures a regular part of WTVT weather.[19] Also in the mid-1960s, George Winterling, of WJXT in Jacksonville, arranged with the National Hurricane Center (by then consolidated in Miami) for spare satellite pictures to be mailed and put on the air each day.[20] While delayed, these shots also let viewers see actual hurricane progress.

Radar displays were another way to increase the visual appeal of weathercasts while showing hurricane behavior. By the late 1950s, a number of coastal television stations had on-site radar transmitters and receivers that could show the distinctive spiral bands of rain associated with hurricanes. Houston's KHOU broadcast live pictures of Hurricane Carla approaching the Texas coast in 1961, with the help of National Weather Service radar in Galveston. Adding to the impact was KHOU's superimposition of a state map over the radar returns. Dan Rather, the CBS anchor then at KHOU, recalled the overlay's effectiveness:

> When I said, "This is actual scale, there's the state of Texas, one inch equals fifty miles," you could hear people in the studio gasp. Anyone with eyes could measure the size of it.[21]

"Live, from the Coast..."

On-the-scene reports are a staple of television news, and no less so for hurricanes. The lead time of hours or even days between hurricane warning and landfall makes it relatively easy to send reporters to the sites expecting greatest damage. Equipment for such remote reporting was bulky and expensive through the 1970s, but that failed to stop many stations. For example, 16 cameramen were placed along the northeast Florida coast by Jacksonville's WFGA to cover Hurricane Dora in 1964. Five years later, as Hurricane Camille approached New Orleans, WDSU supplied an amphibious car to protect reporters heading for the predicted landfall site.[22]

Such ambitious hurricane reporting was then limited to cities in or near a storm's path, due to expense and logistics. By 1980, smaller, more portable cameras made storm reporting easier. Satellite transmission in the mid-1980s further expanded possibilities. Now, even landlocked stations could dispatch a camera crew to Florida to cover hurricanes "live," at relatively little cost. In turn, coastal stations began to cover storms thousands of miles away. Miami's WSUN featured live reports in 1988 from Jamaica, Grand Cayman Island, Mexico, and Texas, all on the progress of

For 36 continuous hours, George Winterling kept viewers of WJXT (Jacksonville) apprised on Hurricane Cleo as the storm moved up Florida's east coast on August 27-28, 1964. (Courtesy WJXT)

Hurricane Gilbert — a storm that remained hundreds of miles from Florida.[23] (The flip side of using remote reporters is that invariably some wind up in a region where the weather is calm. Dozens of stories were filed on Gilbert from Galveston — where it hardly rained during the entire event.)

When a hurricane actually bears down, television stations have traditionally gone to near-continuous coverage of the storm threat. This saturation treatment became more a rarity in the 1980s as station budgets tightened and the loss of advertising revenue due to preempted programs became too burdensome. Public taste seems to have shifted as well, in favor of quick, frequent updates rather than nonstop hurricane news.

In the 1950s and 1960s, though, it was not uncommon for stations to devote entire days of programming to a storm. Dan Rather spent more than 70 hours at the Galveston NWS office covering Hurricane Carla in 1961. Rather later said of KHOU's coverage: "It's real community service. We saved a lot of people and a lot of property by showing just how bad the hurricane was."[24] Rather's stint also boosted his career. CBS noticed the Carla coverage and hired him only months later.

Gloria and the Media

Though hurricane forecasts have continued to improve from the 1960s onward, they are far from perfect. Landfall for most storms still cannot be pinpointed a day in advance any closer than some 100 miles. That blunt fact, standing in contrast to vast improvements in television-weather graphics, has made the National Hurricane Center (NHC) vulnerable to accusations of incompetence. The inevitable public scolding came in 1985 with an especially tricky storm, and the critic was none other than Dan Rather.

America's northeast coast was in that year enjoying the continuation of a remarkably calm period. No serious hurricanes had threatened since 1960. Several powerful storms struck the Gulf states in the early 1980s, but with few deaths or injuries. The National Hurricane Center expanded its media profile greatly during these threats, accommodating the dozens of local reporters who flocked to the center for information. NHC Director Neil Frank became a familiar face on local and national newscasts with live interviews and storm updates.

This informal arrangement between the Hurricane Center and television was tested to its limits during Hurricane Gloria's rampage in September 1985. Gloria followed nearly the identical track of the 1938 New England hurricane, heading northwest to the Carolinas and then skirting the mid–Atlantic coast before crossing Long Island. However, Gloria moved up the East Coast far more slowly than its 1938 counterpart, which allowed for more time over the cooler North Atlantic and substantial weakening as a result. Natural tides were at low ebb with Gloria's approach, further reducing its damage potential. By landfall on September 27, Gloria's top winds were estimated at 120 MPH — certainly powerful but not unprecedented.

Media interest was another matter. Gloria drew unmatched attention from national and local television, in part because it had broken a record for Atlantic Ocean surface pressure three days earlier. That event caused one forecaster to dub Gloria "the storm of the century," a label that stuck even after Gloria weakened. Yet there was still cause for concern: Gloria was approaching parts of the United States that hadn't seen a full hurricane in 25 years. Even a few hours before landfall, forecasters believed the storm could restrengthen or accelerate. The National Hurricane Center thus refused to back off from its call for large-scale action, noting that "hurricane forecasting skills are not sufficient to predict [Gloria's behavior]" and that continued warnings were "the course of least regret."[25] The entire Atlantic coast from North Carolina to Maine was under a hurricane warning on the evening of September 26.

Both local and national newscasts were fixated on Gloria that day and

Neil Frank is the Ph.D. meteorologist who became a television celebrity as director of the National Hurricane Center. In 1987, Frank became chief meteorologist at KHOU, Houston. (Courtesy KHOU)

the next. Cable News Network and The Weather Channel featured near-continuous coverage of the storm, as did most local stations from Washington to Boston. Interviews with Neil Frank of the NHC were ubiquitous, totaling more than 100 on the 27th alone.[26] Frank estimates he gave more individual live-television feeds that week than anyone else in broadcasting history.

> At about three-thirty in the afternoon, I sat down in a chair, and they had a TV camera there . . . we did three-minute feeds until seven-thirty. I never moved out of that chair. All I knew was "You're in Boston, and you're talking to Jean," or "You're in Dallas, and you're talking to Joe."[27]

By midday on the 27th, it was becoming clear that Gloria was not to be a repeat of the 1938 hurricane. The stretch of north-south coastline from New York to Washington experienced high seas and wind, but little structural damage. In all, eight people died and $1 billion in damage occurred;[28] Long Island was hardest hit. But from the vantage point of reporters stationed elsewhere, it appeared that the National Hurricane Center had blown Gloria far out of proportion. The lack of widespread injury, even on Long Island, could have been viewed as the successful outcome of NHC warnings and media focus. Instead, the NHC was accused of *overwarning*. Since the disaster deemed possible had not materialized, critics felt that the disruption of everyday life had been unnecessary.

This reaction was epitomized that evening on the "CBS Evening News" as Dan Rather scolded Neil Frank for overstating Gloria's threat. "He came on and said, 'Are you messing around too much with TV and not paying attention to what you're doing?'" recalls Frank. He adds:

> The next day I got in an airplane, flew over Fire Island, and took pictures of all these places out there that were destroyed . . . but by that time, you know, I couldn't go back to Dan Rather on the CBS news and say, "This is what I told you took place out there."[29]

The wrath directed toward the National Hurricane Center following Gloria didn't last long or change policy much. In 1988, Hurricane Gilbert became the strongest Atlantic storm on record, even topping Gloria. Gilbert seemed especially threatening in that summer's context of a severe Midwest drought and concern over global climate change. Once again, all eyes turned toward the NHC, where the new director, Robert Sheets, granted a record 450 interviews between September 13 and 16.[30] "That kind of approach will continue," said Sheets of the intense coverage started by Frank. "It is ingrained in the system."[31]

As for Sheets' predecessor, Neil Frank accepted early retirement from the NHC in 1987. He then took a job as chief weathercaster for KHOU in Houston, the same station that gave Dan Rather his big break covering Hurricane Carla.

TORNADOES ON TELEVISION

No other phenomenon has posed such a challenge to weathercasting as the violent, fleeting tornado. By their very short-lived nature, tornadoes are hard to detect and to warn against. By the time one is spotted, reported to law-enforcement agencies or the National Weather Service, and mentioned on television, the funnel has often finished its work on earth and retreated into its parent thunderstorm.

The daunting task of tornado coverage on television has inspired some stations to excellence and driven others to resignation. A few weather-casting teams, mostly in the tornado-prone Midwest and plains states, devote much energy to fine-tuning their response to Weather Service bulletins. Their mission is to air tornado warnings minutes or even seconds after issuance. But dozens of other stations cover tornadoes and severe thunderstorms haphazardly, sometimes missing warnings altogether late at night or on weekends. Tornado coverage is indeed a proving ground for the resourcefulness and dedication of weathercasters.

A Tale of Two Twisters

Television of the late 1940s was scarcely equipped to warn the public against tornadoes, as twister forecasting itself was locked in a decades-long inertia. The U.S. Weather Bureau still effectively banned any mention of tornadoes by its local offices, even though hundreds of spotter networks formed during World War II had achieved success in warning military bases of approaching twisters. The most any public or private forecaster could do was to inform relevant agencies of a tornadic situation. Kansas City's Weather Bureau occasionally notified the local Red Cross if a storm outbreak was expected, and radio weathercaster Jim Fidler did the same for news directors at his Midwest stations. Yet public warnings for specific tornadoes were still absent nationwide.

How much of an opportunity was being lost? On April 10, 1947, a huge tornadic storm crossed over 221 miles of Texas, Oklahoma, and Kansas during five hours. Deaths were reported in several communities along the path; almost 100 people were killed and 3,000 rendered homeless in Woodward, Oklahoma. Although the tornado-bearing storm was mentioned to telephone operators in Woodward 15 to 30 minutes before the twister struck, no warnings were passed along to townspeople.[32]

Just as serious as the lack of immediate tornado warnings in 1947 was the absence of large-scale alerts hinting when tornadoes might be possible. Some of the weather factors associated with tornadoes had been known for decades, but this knowledge had not been organized in a useful fashion. The long-delayed breakthrough in tornado forecasting finally came in 1948, thanks largely to a freak recurrence of twisters.

Tinker Air Force Base, a key military installation just southeast of Oklahoma City, was struck on March 20, 1948, by a powerful tornado. Fifty planes were destroyed at a cost of $10 million. Major E. J. Fawbush and Captain Robert Miller, two air force meteorologists at Tinker, took interest in the storm and began work immediately. Within days, the two had come up with a set of guidelines that used upper- and lower-level weather conditions to gauge tornado likelihood. It didn't take long for a test case to occur. On March 25, the chosen criteria pointed to a strong chance of tornadoes in central Oklahoma. Fawbush and Miller informed Tinker staff; planes were put into shelter; and, as if by clockwork, a tornado struck Tinker that evening. This time, damages were greatly reduced by the warning. The first modern tornado prediction was thus a success.[33]

Unlike the hapless work of J. P. Finley in the 1880s, the Fawbush-Miller tornado-prediction scheme aroused immediate interest in Washington. The pair was asked by the U.S. Weather Bureau to spend a year refining their system in private, using actual storm cases from throughout the central United States. That 1949 work further verified the accuracy of the

Fawbush-Miller method. Results were presented to considerable acclaim at the 1950 meeting of the American Meteorological Society.[34] Since Fawbush and Miller were still military men, the Weather Bureau began planning its own severe-weather forecasting center to open in Washington in 1952.

Up to this point, television had been virtually untouched by the rapid progress in tornado forecasting. The 1950 AMS meeting triggered the first mass-media reports on Fawbush and Miller's system. Curiosity grew, especially in Oklahoma. Even as test predictions were being made at Tinker, they remained within the military system; public forecasts were still devoid of any mention of tornadoes. Oklahoma City's sole television station, WKY (now KTVY), became especially interested in the secret warnings. At one point, recalls former WKY weathercaster Harry Volkman, the station was discreetly sending reporters to Tinker in hopes of gleaning information.[35]

Two Weather Bureau developments in March 1952 opened the door to television's first tornado bulletins. F. W. Reichelderfer, then chief of the bureau, established a center in Washington to adapt the Fawbush-Miller technique for civilian use, the first step toward modern tornado watches. Also in that month, Reichelderfer traveled to a number of Midwest cities to institute local warning systems.[36] In Oklahoma City, Reichelderfer met with WKY personnel and local Weather Service forecasters. The upshot of that conference: WKY was granted permission to use Tinker Field tornado predictions on the air.

Still unsure of how the public might react, the station forged ahead. Harry Volkman issued the first televised tornado forecast later that spring. The results, dreaded by so many for so long, could hardly have been more innocuous. No deaths or serious injuries occurred from the ensuing storms, and no panic was reported. On the contrary, hundreds of letters of gratitude poured into WKY during the next weeks, thanking the station for its venture.[37] The prevailing attitude was summarized in one woman's comment, reprinted in *TV Guide:* "We breathe a sigh of relief knowing you are on the job. God bless you."[38]

Watching and Warning

Progress in tornado awareness accelerated from that point on. The fledgling severe-weather-forecast branch of the Weather Bureau was moved to Kansas City in 1954 and christened the National Severe Storms Forecast Center (NSSFC). By then, it was becoming clear that a hierarchy of tornado-awareness bulletins was needed. The Fawbush-Miller criteria were designed to target broad areas (e.g., 100 by 200 miles) in which tornadoes might occur during a two- to six-hour period. Pinpointing a specific tornado that far in advance was still beyond the Weather Bureau's ability. However, local

Weather Bureau offices did receive tornado sightings, and some twisters could be spotted on radar if the characteristic "hook" echo was present. These tornado clues called for a more forthright, immediate alert, covering one or two counties and lasting perhaps 30 minutes.

In the mid-1950s, a multi-tiered system was established by the NSSFC for tornadoes and severe thunderstorms, comparable to the National Hurricane Center's hierarchy for tropical storms. The system was still in use through the 1980s.

- Regular local forecasts continued to omit the word *tornado,* though "possibly severe" thunderstorms could be noted.
- Tornado and severe thunderstorm *watches* were issued from the Kansas City NSSFC, which monitored the entire United States for Fawbush-Miller criteria and sent the watch bulletins to affected areas.
- Tornado *warnings* were issued by local Weather Bureau offices upon public reports or radar indications of tornadoes in the region.[39]

Radio and television were quick to accept the watch-warning format, though not without difficulty. Alliteration in the words *watch* and *warning* led to a fair degree of confusion between the two. Moreover, much of the public, and some broadcasters, were prone to substitute either *watch* or *warning* with the generic term *alert.* Despite these semantic flaws, the National Weather Service has kept the same terminology for over three decades. That sheer continuity has reduced confusion, especially in the most tornado-prone areas.

Most television stations had standardized procedures for handling severe-weather bulletins by the 1960s. Tornado and severe-thunderstorm watches were typically displayed on station-ID display cards and shown every half hour during commercial breaks. In the case of warnings, stations opted to use either *crawls* or *cut-ins.* Crawls are a method of running pertinent information across the bottom of the television screen (see Chapter 5); cut-ins interrupted programs for a mini-weathercast, complete with maps, radar display, and a weather anchor speaking for perhaps 30 seconds.

Some stations went all out for severe-weather coverage. After a brush with killer storms in 1964, Minneapolis' KSTP built its "Emergency Weather Center."[40] As described in *Television Age,* "A separate studio, complete with weather charts, lights, audio and video . . . is ready at all times. A push of a button cuts out regular programming and cuts in the [KSTP] Emergency Weather Center." Another way to improve severe-storm coverage was radar; the device had become standard equipment through the plains and Midwest by 1970.

As early as 1955, Jim Fidler (then at Cincinnati's WLWT) made radar a staple of his severe-weather coverage. The actual radar display is at lower right. (Courtesy Jim Fidler)

Unlike hurricane threats, which might extend over a period of days, severe storms affect smaller regions for a shorter time. Continuous severe-weather coverage has thus been extremely rare, reserved for a period of perhaps one hour at the height of a storm, or longer in the aftermath of catastrophic damage. Following the Palm Sunday tornado outbreak of 1965, Indianapolis' WFBM canceled all regular programs for two days to relay information on relief efforts, victims' names, and so on.[41] (As with hurricanes, this type of intensive coverage became less frequent in the cost-conscious 1980s.)

High drama can erupt on the television screen when tornadoes approach. A huge twister bore down on Topeka, Kansas, on the night of June 8, 1966. As the storm neared town, WIBW anchorman Bill Kurtis told his audience, "If you're not under cover now, for God's sake, take cover!" The station's 25-minute advance warning was credited with helping keep the death toll to 17, despite 500 injuries and $100 million in damage.[42]

There is plentiful evidence that the public takes televised tornado warnings quite seriously. A 1984 survey in Oklahoma City found that 80 percent of respondents considered television their first choice for severe-

Before computer graphics existed, Jim Williams used hand-drawn maps to display tornado watch areas and thunderstorm locations at WKY (now KTVY), Oklahoma City. (Courtesy KTVY)

weather information.[43] Several other studies back up this figure, though most have been conducted in the Midwest and plains states where tornadoes are most frequent. In other parts of the country, warnings often seem to be handled with less urgency. For example, Miami's WSUN rarely broke into programming for tornado warnings in the late 1980s, preferring to use crawls. Weathercaster Bob Soper, of WSUN, noted the weakness and frequency of waterspouts in the Miami area as a factor in the station's choice to deemphasize tornado warnings.[44]

Another crucial element in severe-weather coverage is the distance of storm threats from a television station. Among station managers surveyed by the National Association of Broadcasters in 1978 on their watch and warning transmissions, most reported they were less likely to interrupt programming for severe thunderstorm or tornado warnings the farther those threats were from their station.[45]

Tornado warnings seem destined to become more prominent on television in the 1990s and beyond. The National Weather Service is planning a major upgrade of its radar systems that will bring Doppler-radar coverage to most of the United States. These radars have been shown to give up to 20 minutes' advance warning of intense tornadoes. Several dozen television stations had acquired their own Dopplers by the mid-1980s, making some weathercasters as well equipped as their local Weather Service meteorologists to spot tornadoes on radar.[46] Oklahoma City's KWTV has not been hesitant to issue tornado warnings independent of the NWS through its own Doppler radar and to trumpet those successes in promotional ads (see Chapter 3). Even stations that are unable to buy Dopplers may eventually display Doppler output through cooperative arrangements with the NWS. The graphic appeal of such displays and their improved lead time could increase the use of cut-ins for tornado warnings nationwide, reducing deaths and injuries.

FLASH FLOODS: THE WEAKEST LINK

Despite the greater attention given to tornadoes and hurricanes, flash floods emerged as the most consistently deadly weather phenomenon in America during the 1970s and 1980s. Flood waters annually kill over 100 people, many of whom are trapped while seeking false safety in their automobiles.

This weather killer has been ignored by television for decades. Even stations that devote endless energy to covering tornadoes or hurricanes often neglect to warn viewers about flooding. A 1987 study of weather advisories on Oklahoma City television found that flash-flood warnings were broadcast up to 2½ hours after issuance by the National Weather Service.[47] Since flood conditions can change by the second, these late warnings have questionable value.

Not all of the burden falls on television. The complexities of estimating rainfall and riverflow make flash-flood warnings a difficult task for the Weather Service. For example, a rampaging Big Thompson River killed 139 people in Colorado on the state's centennial in 1976. Most of the victims died before the seriousness of the situation was publicized;[48] radar returns had been attenuated by mountains and failed to indicate huge downpours.

Another problem in flash-flood safety is the automobile. Televised warnings cannot reach people trying to cross high water in their cars, the act resulting in most flood deaths. Radio messages can be vital at this point. (Postflood coverage can also make a difference. The Fort Collins station KCOL received a special award from the American Meteorological Society for its emergency broadcasts both during and after the Big Thompson flood.)[49]

Technology may once again come to the rescue in flood warning. The NWS Doppler network planned for the 1990s will include sophisticated computer programs to provide early warning of flood-prone situations. Perhaps a concerted effort from the Weather Service to publicize and improve on flash-flood warnings will produce the same in-depth television coverage that hurricane and tornado events now enjoy.

9

Radio Weather

For a medium whose influence peaked some 50 years ago, radio has held its place in American culture with remarkable tenacity. Television may be able to keep an audience more firmly than its audio counterpart, but radio is more subtly and thoroughly woven into the fabric of daily living. People will sit before a television set for hours watching a movie or baseball game, yet radio listeners tune into their favorite station while driving, reading, working, relaxing, or even bathing. The pocket-size transistor radios of the 1960s and the portable headphones of the 1980s have taken the medium virtually anywhere its audience cares to go.

If people use radio as their information source when out and about, what better way to tell them about the weather they'll be experiencing? Radio's role in covering weather can be just as important as television's. While TV has the visuals needed to explain and educate most effectively, a radio voice is perfectly adequate for nitty-gritty weather details: temperature, humidity, wind speed. During severe weather, radios can be operated even if electric power is lost. And while music has been the core element of radio programming since the 1950s, weather reports are more listened to than their brevity might indicate. A Gallup Poll commissioned for NBC in 1977 found that weather news was the single most important factor among the listeners polled in choosing a radio station.[1] That criterion seems remarkably stable: a 1987 Associated Press poll came up with similar results.[2]

With fewer dollars to spend than their television counterparts, radio stations are forced to be ingenious in their weather coverage. The result is a vast spectrum of quantity and quality. Stations may opt for practically no weather coverage, dutifully read only the official data and forecasts, contract with a private forecasting service for daily reports, or hire a meteorologist to work full- or part-time for that station alone.

THE BASIC APPROACH

Whether big or small, devoted to classical music or rock, most radio stations adhere to a few conventions of weather reporting. Some of these traditions are outlined in a 1981 report commissioned by the National Weather Service (NWS). Personnel at nine radio stations in the Northeast were surveyed, representing markets as big as Philadelphia (WCAU) and as small as Georgetown, Delaware (WJWL).

"Drive time" — the early-morning and late-afternoon hours when most workers commute to and from their jobs — is the peak period for radio weather. Reports during drive time typically include a short-term forecast (for the next few hours) along with current conditions. In large metropolitan areas, they may be delivered with traffic conditions and oriented to crosstown differences (e.g., "heavy rain on the north side, tapering off as you approach downtown"). The Weather Service team found morning drive-time updates lasting from 1 to 1½ minutes and broadcast every six to ten minutes. At the top of each hour, in-depth coverage lasted up to three minutes. During the evening drive time, reports were similar in length but slightly less frequent.[3]

Radio weather coverage is more sporadic outside of commuting periods. During the workday, reports on most stations are spaced 15 to 30 minutes apart. These are commonly "rip and read" updates; disc jockeys simply take weather information off the station teletype and repeat it on the air, perhaps adding a temperature reading from the station thermometer if one exists. From late evening until morning, reports are even less frequent, averaging once or twice per hour at stations surveyed by the Weather Service.[4] Again, "rip and read" is the usual strategy, since few radio stations have newspeople on duty at these late (or very early) hours.

How can stations that rely on teletype improve their weather reports? One tool is language. The NWS found stations leaning away from dry statistics toward more colorful descriptive terms — *breezy, muggy*. Another trick is to relate the official forecast to listeners' activities. Besides the commuter tie-in described above, stations might key their updates to boating, baseball games, or outdoor concerts.[5] Of course, these references must be quick and concise in a one-minute weathercast; usually, they provide a lead-in to a verbatim reading of the NWS forecast and local conditions.

ALTERNATIVES

For a good number of radio stations, especially those in large cities or boasting large audiences, "rip and read" isn't enough. Six of the nine stations surveyed by the Weather Service in 1980 availed themselves of private

Francis Davis did both radio and television weathercasting for WFIL, Philadelphia, from the late 1940s onward. (Courtesy *Bulletin of the American Meteorological Society*)

meteorologists, whether in-house or through an external company.[6] The reports are often similar in timing, length, and substance to the NWS forecast, but delivery from a bona fide weathercaster gives them an authority lacking in disc jockeys or even regular radio newspeople.

Going It Alone: In-House Weathercasters

Paying for a meteorologist might at first glance seem a burdensome expense for any radio station. Who needs a "real" weatherperson when no maps can be pointed to, no costumes worn? Nevertheless, a small but distinct set of radio outlets choose to hire their own weathercasters. Their investment pays off in flexible and detailed weather reporting, especially during severe weather.

Though announcers gave weather on experimental radio as early as World War I, it was the radio boom of the early 1920s that gave the medium its first bona fide weathercaster, E. B. Rideout of WEEI, one of Boston's first stations. Rideout's daily reports, sponsored by H. B. Hood Milk Producers, were broadcast from the 1920s through the early 1960s — remarkable longevity, considering the changes in radio and society as a whole during that period. "He was very straightforward," recalls Norm Macdonald, a listener in the 1930s who was inspired by Rideout to take up weathercasting himself.[7]

Television weathercaster Harry Spohn (KNOP, North Platte) records an update for early-morning radio.

Other pioneering weathercasters took to the airwaves in the 1930s and 1940s: Jim Fidler, of WLBC in Muncie, Indiana (and later WLW in Cincinnati); Don Kent, of Boston's WBZ; and James Reid, of the TN network in North Carolina. The first two men went to television in the 1950s, but Kent continued doing radio weather in New England, even after retiring from televsion in the 1980s.[8] James Reid was posthumously honored by the American Meteorological Society in 1973 for his "How's the Weather" series, which ran for over 30 years.[9]

As television weather drifted into comic superficiality during the 1950s, radio weathercasting came on similar hard times. Predictions of radio's demise were widespread, and few young meteorologists could bypass the promise of television in favor of a presumably dying medium. Not everyone gave up on radio, though. The American Meteorological Society paralleled its television seal of approval program with a similar seal for radio weathercasters beginning in 1959. The roster of early sealholders in radio includes a large number from private forecasting firms (see page 125), along with independents such as Eugene Grueber, of KHAS, Hastings, Nebraska.[10]

Ironically, the boom in private companies doing radio weather in the late 1960s and 1970s helped the cause of independent weathercasters. Firms such as Accu-Weather often stipulated that only one station per market could use their services. That left the hiring of a full-time meteorologist as one way for other stations to compete with private weathercasting firms.

Another option was for stations to contract with a local television weathercaster for moonlighting duty. For example, a morning weather-caster might telephone the radio station from his television studio with short drive-time outlooks, then record midmorning updates to be broad-cast each hour. Since television and radio don't compete directly with one another, these arrangements were often surprisingly easy to make. The cross-promotion between outlets made such deals appealing to both par-ties. Of course, some companies own radio and television stations sharing the same home city and call letters (such as Boston's WBZ), which made sharing weathercasters even simpler.

Kirk Melhuish: Starting a Radio Career

Even with the influx of television weathercasters pulling extra duty on radio, there was room in the late 1980s for the occasional person seeking only a full-time radio slot. One such person was Kirk Melhuish, who became the sole meteorologist for WSB in Atlanta while only in his mid-twenties.[11] (Few meteorologists begin television work at that age in a city the size of Atlanta.)

Melhuish gained experience in both radio and television while attend-ing Valparaiso University in the early 1980s. By the time he joined WSB in 1987, he had reported weather for five radio and two television stations. WSB's radio weather had been handled by a meteorologist for WSB-TV un-til the radio station's news director decided that "we needed our own weather authority on a day-to-day basis."[12]

Morning and evening drive times are the focus for WSB weather-casting. Melhuish works a split shift, giving live reports during both com-muting periods and taping broadcasts for the midday hours. In a 1987 inter-view, he commented on the importance placed on his duties by listeners:

> There is a huge interest in solid weather information, second only to news and followed by traffic. The station could have gone with long-distance ser-vices I call McWeather, but these services don't know the city first hand. I'm onsite, and I can devote my full attention to the weather.[13]

What some might see as the limitations of radio are advantages to Melhuish, who appreciates the generous time allotted for his show.

> When the data comes in, I can put it on the air immediately. I don't have to play with my computer crayon to make the proper map or chart for it and wait for the next scheduled newscast to come up.[14]

Having more time to fill each day also gives Melhuish a chance to clown, in spite of his businesslike approach when handling weather itself.

Kirk Melhuish (Courtesy WSB radio, Atlanta).

> With a three- and four-hour show, there's plenty of room for goofing
> around and for developing yourself as a personality, yet still maintaining
> the integrity of the information you provide.[15]

In striving for both humor and respect, Melhuish has achieved a successful balance. *Atlanta Magazine* named him the city's favorite weathercaster in 1989 over competitors from both radio and television. As for his
scientific peers, the National Weather Association gave Melhuish Radio
Meteorologist of the Year honors in 1988 for a five-day advance prediction
of a snowstorm.[16]

FRANCHISE FORECASTING: THE PRIVATE FIRMS

What kind of company could be called, as Kirk Melhuish put it, a
McWeather service? Several firms qualified for that title in the 1980s. Like
the popular restaurant chain McDonald's, these companies turn out a
dependable, familiar product. In their case, the product is weather coverage tailored to specific locales but produced and distributed from a central
point. These "franchise forecasts" have all the merits and shortfalls of any
mass-produced item. While their accuracy is often above reproach, it
comes with the loss of local flavor and detail, and the addition of a certain
dubious intimacy.

The business potential of weathercasting for multiple markets was obvious even before television began to intrude on radio. In the 1930s, Salvatore Pagliuca pioneered multistation weather reports through the Yankee Network, based at Boston's WNAC. Pagliuca collected observations from the network's radio outlets throughout New England and incorporated them into two 15-minute shows each day.[17] While at Cincinnati's WLW in 1940, Jim Fidler broadcast hurricane bulletins to oceanic listeners through the shortwave station WLWO, even translating the advisories into Spanish and Portuguese when appropriate.[18]

Still, these services were courtesy of full-time weathercasters based at single large stations. The first step toward consolidating weathercast resources outside a media outlet took place in 1946, with Marion Hogan's founding of Weather Services, Inc., in Bedford, Massachusetts.[19] The company grew to become a powerhouse in providing forecasts for media as well as industry.* The company became Weather Services Corporation after merging with Northeast Weather Service in 1969.[20] In 1985, the firm's 40 meteorologists prepared daily tape-recorded weathercasts for over 50 radio stations. The company also prepared maps and data for the newspaper *USA Today* and served such clients as Coca-Cola, IBM, and Union Carbide.[21]

Following in the footsteps of WSC was Travelers Weather Service (TWS), based at the headquarters of the Travelers Insurance Companies in Hartford, Connecticut. This subsidiary of the Travelers was founded after the string of New England hurricanes in 1954–1955. It grew quickly, serving media and industry; its staff of meteorologists collected seven of the first ten seals granted to radio weathercasters. (Those seals are credited to WTIC, the television station in Hartford then owned by the Travelers.) After new management at the Travelers lost interest in its weather forecasting service in the 1970s, it splintered into several groups.[22]

Another heavyweight joined the ranks of private weathercasting with Accu-Weather's creation in 1962. Founder Dr. Joel Myers started the company as a ski-forecasting service for resorts in the Northeast. The town he selected as the location of his new company was an appropriate choice: State College, Pennsylvania, is nestled in the Allegheny Mountains and supports Pennsylvania State University, with its large and distinguished school of meteorology.

It took only a decade for Accu-Weather to branch from ski outlooks into prepackaged forecasts for media. In 1978, 65 radio and television

---

*Weather Services Corporation is often confused with WSI Corporation. The latter began as a subsidiary of the former, focusing on weather data access, in 1978. WSI was sold in 1983 and remains a major source of packaged data and graphics (see Chapter 5), while Weather Services is primarily a forecasting company. Both are located in Bedford, Mass.

stations used Accu-Weather services.[23] By 1989, that total had risen to 120 radio and 200 television outlets. Meeting those commitments were 75 full-time meteorologists; about half of these were featured on the air at client stations, the rest working behind the scenes.[24]

The Accu-Weather format, already well developed by this point, was straightforward. Around 45 minutes before a client's newscast, forecasters phoned that station with the morning (or evening) update. The outlook was then taped by the station for replay during the newscast. Some stations, preferring more spontaneity and interplay, featured the Accu-Weather forecast as a live part of their news.[25]

With either option, the result was a recognizable Accu-Weather segment. Forecasts were delivered in a bright manner, with tight, pithy language: "Today, mixed clouds and sun. High thirty-five. Tonight, snow likely early, tapering off by dawn. Low twenty-four." Used for all clients, the Accu-Weather phraseology was designed to be consistent, yet flexible enough for subtle weather distinctions. "We've tried to upgrade communication used by the National Weather Service and other private forecasters," says Myers. "We felt the NWS was stuck in jargon from fifty or so years ago. We use the journalists' tools and communicate weather using the English language."[26]

Another distinctive part of the Accu-Weather approach, and perhaps its biggest departure from old-fashioned weathercasting, is its underplaying of the distance between the forecaster and his or her audience. Even when giving a live update from Pennsylvania to listeners in Texas, for example, the Accu-Weather style is to say, "Here in Dallas, *we* expect..." or "*We* had some sunshine today..." While some listeners might know that Accu-Weather isn't based in their hometown, others might take the statements at face value and assume the weathercaster is actually "here in Dallas."

Whatever the semantics of long-distance weathercasting, its substance can rank high in quality. For most areas and most types of weather situations, a forecast need not be locally produced to be accurate. Virtually all of the needed data is available through the National Weather Service and its nationwide satellite and teletype links. Severe weather poses more of a challenge for distant forecasting companies since warnings are issued by local National Weather Service offices. A station with on-site meteorologists can usually air such bulletins more quickly, and listeners may phone in to provide the weathercaster with added detail. Local meteorologists are also more familiar with regional influences such as the "Denver convergence zone" that often produces tornadoes near that city.

Even for severe storms, Accu-Weather can provide better coverage than a teletype alone. "We have access to radars that cover about ninety-five percent of the country," says senior meteorologist Jim Candor. "We can see the big storms just as easily as someone who's sitting there [at the radio station]." In threatening situations, Accu-Weather will contact a station and either break in with live updates or let the station notify viewers, depending on client preference.[27]

Starting a Forecast Service: Ed St. Pé

Though the biggest players in "franchise forecasting" got started early, the 1980s boom in technology for receiving weather data opened the doors for other ambitious people. One of the many smaller companies that attained regional influence during the later 1980s was Ed St. Pé's National Weather Network.

Ironically, St. Pé got his start in media weather the old-fashioned way—as a television anchor in Baton Rouge, Louisiana. When St. Pé decided to try forming a radio forecast service, his station was not only amenable but enthusiastic toward the idea. A bartering system resulted whereby radio stations in the Baton Rouge television market could receive St. Pé's weathercasts in exchange for advertising. By 1987, the state of Louisiana was "saturated" with 25 client stations for St. Pé. "There wasn't much opportunity to grow," he told *Small Market Radio Newsletter,* "so we decided to expand outside the state." A year later, 20 more stations had joined the National Weather Network, in regions as far away as central Illinois and northern Florida.[28]

St. Pé's service exemplified one of the crucial selling points of contracted weathercasts: A smaller station could add personality and authority to its weather segments without the expense of hiring an on-site meteorologist. In 1987, St. Pé charged clients $125 per month for three updates per day, with the station paying phone tolls of perhaps $75 a month. Extra updates were provided at no cost during severe weather:

> "Believe it or not," said St. Pé, "most of the time when we call with one of those severe weather bulletins, it's the first anybody has heard about it.... Having voiced weather forecasts gives a station real credibility, and those reports are easy to sell.[29]

Idealistic souls who see weathercasting as a public service might not care for the bottom-line business orientation of St. Pé, Accu-Weather, and other private forecasters. Yet, like any successful business venture, these options are filling a real need. Weathercasters are an institution on television, but they can be found on only a few radio stations. If radio is to match television in weathercasting support, station owners must be convinced that giving tomorrow's forecast in a personal way is not only good for listeners but good for business.

10

Tomorrow's Outlook

What next for television weather? Have millions of two-minute segments exhausted every possible cliché, used every possible technique to spruce up a forecast of "partly cloudy and warmer"? Or will technology save the day, bringing new graphics and formats to the genre?

The prognosis given by some weathercasters in the late 1980s was gloomy. There was a sense that weathercasting as a specialty of television news was doomed, that it was seen by station management as an increasingly expensive and dispensable part of the newscast. Though few if any stations have succeeded in disposing with the traditional weathercast, the fear of such action remains. Another concern among television meteorologists is that their expertise will simply be made irrelevant. Flashy graphics and prepackaged forecasts make it easier than ever for a speaker to communicate weather without understanding it.

Valerie Voss, of the Cable News Network, sees trouble in the loss of meteorologists from television weather:

> To get a fine broadcaster and communicator who also looks good and moves well and speaks well, sometimes management is willing to forgo the credentials.... I'm worried about that. I see a lot of people on television giving out misinformation. They're just wrong about what they're saying.[1]

As creator of The Weather Channel, a truly innovative venture, John Coleman knows the unexpected paths weathercasting can take. Coleman doesn't see the end of television weather so much as its removal from traditional local news and a subsequent shift to pay-as-you-go, individualized weather data available from home phone or computer.

> I don't see TV weather having a great future in the format in which it exists, because of the attitude that weather is a trivial piece of the television

129

newscast. Less and less emphasis is given to it by most stations. . . . News departments' budgets are generally being greatly reduced [because of financial constraints on noncable TV], and in the process, the emphasis on weather is diminishing. The attitude is "Well, there's a weather channel to serve this trivial need, and it's not a big ratings factor for us. Let's de-emphasize it."

I would not be surprised if, a decade from now . . . the weathercast is no longer a part of the newscast. There'll be weather-news stories, but there won't be a weathercast. Rather, that will be relegated to The Weather Channel or a weather dial-up service.[2]

Perhaps Coleman's vision will prove accurate. However, another school of thought holds that the weathercaster is more than a purveyor of dry facts. He or she, whether comic or serious, serves as a personal link to the unknown, at once concerned with the tangible (today's weather) and the mysterious (tomorrow's weather). We may laugh at a weatherman for missing yesterday's forecast, but we listen when he talks about the next day. What better sign of this exists than the prototypical happy-talk interchange in which the news anchor praises or scorns the weathercaster based on the day's conditions ("Well, Jack, you gave us some beautiful sunshine today. Can you do it again tomorrow?"). It remains to be seen whether a computer-generated outlook, no matter how efficient, can replace a human-delivered outlook.

Beyond their role as soothsayers, weathercasters traditionally bring a relaxed element to the newscast, a touch of informality. Most weather anchors, even the ones serious about forecasting, go along with this expectation to some extent, joking and laughing before their reports if not during them. Others, like Willard Scott, make entertainment the central theme.

Why does the very serious topic of weather continue to be treated with such frivolity? One reason may be the public's view of meteorology as something less than a true science. Most scientists conduct repeated experiments in the privacy of a lab before going public with theories or findings. Weather forecasters have no such luxury; their assertions are instantly common knowledge, and their lab — the atmosphere — is open to all. When meteorologists miss a forecast, they must answer to a public that already knows the extent of their error. Moreover, the history of weather forecasting is one of slow progress, not the dramatic discoveries that people associate with medicine, for example.

Other factors play into the perennial treatment of weathercasting as a joke, including the need for comic relief after reporting gruesome news stories. As long as weather forecasts remain imperfect, the weather report will provide ample opportunity for poking fun at the deficiencies of forecasting. And humor is a basic human function, one that technology is unlikely to render obsolete.

There's another possibility, though: The weathercast might not stay as it is *or* die out. Instead, it could evolve into an altogether new part of the newscast.

The late 1980s were a period of increasing concern about the impact of humanity on global weather and climate. It seemed not only possible but probable that fossil-fuel burning and other activities were beginning to increase the average global temperature. At the same time, damage to the earth's protective ozone layer was being discovered, which pointed to increased rates of skin cancer and other dire effects.

Jay Rosen, a journalism professor at New York University, finds significance for the weathercast in these trends. According to Rosen, the usual lighthearted weather segment is actually an escape from human-caused problems.

> While the weatherman is sometimes the bearer of bad news, the bad news he brings says nothing about the badness of human nature or the bad deeds of powerful people; . . . the harm that may come to crops, homes, and cities from various weather disasters does not disturb the essential harmlessness of the weather as a topic for television, for the violence the victims suffer is without any social cause.[3]

In Rosen's view, weathercasting could never be the same if it acknowledged that humans were altering the weather itself.

> It will be interesting to see what television does as weather loses its innocence. . . . The happy atmosphere of the weather report will be difficult to maintain, for the weather can no longer serve as a haven from [human] history.[4]

Could the weathercast grow into a broader forum on the environment as a whole? That direction has precedents. Many weathercasters have done science reporting. San Francisco's KGO established a reporting unit called The Naturalists in 1989. This four-person team of weathercasters delved into microclimates of the San Francisco Bay, the ecological history of the bay, and local effects anticipated from global climate change.

In any case, whether television weather confronts or escapes the issue of worldwide change in the atmosphere, the days of a cute cartoon lamb delivering forecasts with a song appear to be long past. As the age of information moves on, it will take weather broadcasting with it, for better or worse.

Appendix I:
Weathercaster Biographies

Below are backgrounds and achievements of a few veteran weathercasters from across the United States. Some of the people responded to a call for information that was published in the *National Weather Association Newsletter* and posted at two AMS Broadcast Meteorology conferences. Others were chosen for their longtime service or for noteworthy accomplishments. Out of perhaps 2,000 weathercasters, the listing below is only a sampling. This section is not intended to be comprehensive but is a reflection of the various kinds of people in weathercasting. The affiliations listed were current as of early 1989.

ALBERT, Dick (Boston). WCVB, 1978-. Received 1987 New England Emmy for outstanding weathercaster. Also, KOA (Denver), 1976-78; KRON (San Francisco), 1975-76; KOB, Albuquerque. Air Force meteorologist, early 1970s. Hosts "Use Your Smarts," entertainment-education series for young people. Bachelor's and master's degrees, University of Michigan. AMS sealholder.

BARTLETT, Joel (San Francisco). KGO, 1989-; KPIX, 1976-89. Meteorologist for Pacific Gas and Electric, 1968-76; Air Force meteorology instructor, 1960s. B.S. in mechanical engineering, Virginia Polytechnic Institute; M.B.A., San Francisco State University. AMS sealholder.

BASKERVILLE, Steve (Chicago, Philadelphia, National). First black network weathercaster. WBBM (Chicago), 1987-. "CBS Morning News," 1984-87. KYW (Philadelphia), 1977-84; also cohosted talk show, hosted children's program at KYW. Began broadcasting career with children's show for the Philadelphia School District Office of Curriculum, 1972–75. B.S. in communications, Temple University.

BECKMAN, Johnny (Atlanta). WXIA, 1982–. Also, WSB (Atlanta), 1962–82; WFGA (Jacksonville), 1957–62; WSJS (Winston-Salem, NC), 1954–57. Recipient of NWS award for excellence in television weathercasting. Attended Appalachian State Teacher's College, majoring in science education.

CAPELL, Jack (Portland, Oregon). KGW, 1956–. NWS forecaster, 1950–56; Bonneville Power Administration meteorologist, 1956–58. Wrote first intensive study of Oregon's Columbus Day 1962 storm. B.S. in meteorology, University of Washington. Recipient of nineteenth AMS seal, first in Pacific Northwest; 1989 AMS Award for Outstanding Service by a Broadcast Meteorologist.

COLEMAN, John (Chicago, National). Founder of The Weather Channel and active local and national weathercaster. WMAQ (Chicago), 1984–. Also on WLS and WBBM (Chicago), WISN (Milwaukee), KETV (Omaha), WMBD (Peoria), and WCIA (Champaign). First weathercaster, "Good Morning America," ABC, 1977–82. Chicago Emmy recipient for WLS series on tornadoes, 1978. AMS Broadcast Meteorologist of the Year, 1983; NWA Broadcast Meteorologist of the Year, 1981.

COPELAND, Bob (Boston). Veteran of New England weather coverage. WCVB, 1972–; WHDH, 1966–72; WBZ, 1957–66. Owner, Minuteman Weather Service, Inc., publisher of *New England Weather Calendar*. Bachelor's degree, Northeastern University; M.S. in meteorology, Massachusetts Institute of Technology. 1982 Outstanding Alumnus Award for Public Service, Northeastern University. Twentieth recipient of AMS seal.

COUGHLIN, John (Chicago). WBBM, 1970–. Weathercaster and active host-announcer of WBBM entertainment programs. Hosted "The Red Jacket," a children's special awarded a Chicago Emmy. Became interested in meteorology while apprenticing with Chicago veteran weathercaster P. J. Hoff. Bachelor's in chemistry and English, Northwestern University. Member, Chicago AMS chapter.

DENARDO, Joe (Pittsburgh). WTAE, 1969–; KDKA, 1960–69. Founded Denardo and McFarland Weather Services, Inc., in 1956. Active in

John Coughlin (WBBM, Chicago). (Courtesy WBBM)

community affairs: cohosts Pittsburgh United Cerebral Palsy Telethon, sponsors Joe Denardo Celebrity Golf Tournament in St. Mary's, Pa. B.A. in math/physics, Duquesne University; M.S. in meteorology, University of Chicago. AMS sealholder; member of Committee of Industrial Meteorologists.

DESHLER, Steve (Chicago, National). WLS, 1980–82 and 1984–. "CBS Morning News," 1982–84. Also, WKRC (Cincinnati), 1978–80; WZKO (Kalamazoo), 1971–78. Hosted "Viewfinder," public-affairs show, while at WZKO. B.A. in communications and English, Western Michigan University.

FIDLER, Jim (Cincinnati, National, Austin). Among the foremost pioneers in radio and television weather. KTBC (Austin), 1971–86. Also, WLWT (Cincinnati), 1954–57; "Today" (through National Weather Service), 1952–54; WLW radio (Cincinnati), 1938–41, 1945–47; WLBC radio (Muncie, Ind.), 1933–38. Honorary AMS sealholder. Air Force weather instructor, World War II. Involved with Weather Service broadcast experiments from 1940s through 1960s. B.S., Ball State University, 1935.

FIELD, Frank (New York). Longest-serving weathercaster in New York. WCBS, 1984–; WNBC, 1957–84. First use of satellite and radar in weather-

Frank Field (WCBS, New York). (Courtesy WCBS)

casts of the Northeast. Weather Bureau meteorologist, 1940s and 1950s; Air Force weather officer in World War II. B.S. in geology. Doctorate in optometry, State University of New York College of Optometry. AMS sealholder.

FIELD, Storm (New York). Active health reporter–weathercaster, son of New York weathercaster Frank Field. WABC, 1976–; WPIX (science reporting), 1976. Numerous awards for coverage of autism, cancer, cystic fibrosis, etc. Assistant professor, State University of New York College of Optometry. B.A. in history/English, McGill University (Montreal); B.S., doctorate in optometry, Massachusetts College of Optometry. AMS sealholder.

FORRESTER, Frank (Washington). Pioneer meteorologist-weathercaster. WOR (New York), 1949–51; WJXT (Jacksonville), 1957–60; WRC (Washington), 1960s. Left weathercasting to become public information director, U.S. Geological Survey.

FRANK, Neil (Houston). Frequently seen on local and national television while director of the National Hurricane Center, 1974–87. Began at KHOU

Paul Joseph (WTMJ, Milwaukee). (Courtesy WTMJ)

(Houston) upon retirement from NHC in 1987. Trained as Air Force meteorologist. M.S., Ph.D. in meteorology, Florida State University. Elected to AMS National Council, 1989. Numerous papers on tropical meteorology in professional journals.

GIDDINGS, Peter (San Francisco). KGO, 1969–. Also, WSIX (Nashville), 1968–69; WTVT (Tampa), 1963–68. Air Force meteorologist, 1959–63. Recipient of San Francisco Emmy award for "What Makes the Wind Blow" weather special. Active in youth education and service. AMS sealholder; member, AMS Board on School and Popular Meteorologoical and Oceanographic Education.

GIKOFSKY, Irving (New York). WCBS, 1977–. Began weathercasting after long teaching career at Albert Einstein Intermediate School, the Bronx. 1981 Teacher of the Year, New York City Board of Education. Founded "Weatherbreakers," NYC observing network. B.A. in history; M.A. in secondary education, Hofstra University.

JOSEPH, Paul (Milwaukee). WTMJ, 1970–; first meteorologist in market. Also on KUTV (Salt Lake City), 1969. B.S., M.S. in meteorology, University of Utah. AMS seal; served on boards of Broadcast Meteorology and Meteorological Education. Has taught meteorology courses at Marquette University.

LEEP, Roy (Tampa). Pioneer in weathercasting technology. WTVT, 1957–. Heads one of the largest television meteorology staffs in United States. WTVT among first stations to feature regular satellite pictures, lightning detection, computer graphics, color radar. Weather instructor for Air Force, observer for NWS in 1950s. Tenth AMS sealholder; AMS Fellow, served on National Council and Board of Broadcast Meteorology. Director, Gulf Coast Weather Service.

MILHAM, Dan (New Orleans). WDSU, 1977–. AMS sealholder; first-place winner for weathercasting, 1988 UPI Louisiana News Awards. Studied broadcasting at Wayne State University, Detroit, and meteorology through off-campus programs, Pennsylvania State and Mississippi State universities.

MUNSON, Dale (Omaha). WOWT, 1963–. Also, KGLO (Mason City, Iowa), 1957–63. B.A. in speech/journalism, University of Minnesota. Active in Omaha choral organizations. Commended by the Omaha/Offutt chapter of the AMS.

MURRAY, Dave (St. Louis, Boston, National). WBZ (Boston), 1986–. Weathercaster for ABC's "Good Morning America," 1983–86. KSDK (St. Louis), 1976–83. First meteorologist in market since 1950s. B.A. in geography (meteorology specialty), University of Rhode Island; graduate work in atmospheric science, University of Wyoming. Past chairman, AMS Board of Broadcast Meteorology. Author, "The New Murray's Almanac," "The Dangerous Cloud," "Tornadoes – Be Aware."

ROBERTS, Nash, Jr. (New Orleans). "Mr. Weather" of southeast Louisiana, renowned for hurricane coverage. WDSU (1947–73); WVUE (1973–77); WWL (1977–), most recently as consultant during hurricane threats. Trained in aeronautical meteorology, 1939–40; taught meteorology, Loyola University of the South and U.S. Naval Air Station in New Orleans, World War II. Founder, Nash C. Roberts, Jr. Consultants, Inc. Active in literacy campaigns; two terms as president, Louisiana State Board of Education. Thirty-third AMS sealholder.

Harold Taft (KXAS, Fort Worth). (Courtesy KXAS)

RYAN, Bob (Boston, Washington, National). Weathercaster for NBC's "Today," 1978–80; WRC (Washington), 1980– (traded positions with Willard Scott). Also, WCVB (Boston), 1973–78. B.A., M.A. in atmospheric science, State University of New York–Albany. Member, American Association for the Advancement of Science. AMS sealholder; has served on Committee for Broadcast Meteorology and for Professional Affairs.

SCHWOEGLER, Bruce (Boston). WBZ, 1968–. Winner, first New England Emmy for outstanding weathercaster, 1986. Environmental consultant, Museum of Science in Boston. Faculty member, Boston University. Author, *Weather and Energy* (McGraw-Hill, 1982); environmental columnist, United Press International (1983–86); Associated Press (1986–). Navy meteorologist in Alaska and Florida, 1960s. Member, AMS Board of School and Popular Meteorological and Oceanographic Education.

STEFFEN, Bill (Grand Rapids, Michigan). WZZM, 1974–. Has delivered over 1,000 speeches to schools, church groups, civic clubs. Remained at WZZM studios for 3½ days during blizzard of 1978. B.S. in meteorology, University of Wisconsin. AMS sealholder.

TAFT, Harold (Dallas–Fort Worth). The longest-serving United States weathercaster at a single station. KXAS, 1949– (formerly WBAP); also weathercaster for WBAP radio, 1946-. Air Force weather officer, 1942-76; American Airlines meteorologist, 1946-64. A.B. in math and physics and graduate work, Air Force Technical Institute for Meteorology.

THOMPSON, Mark (San Francisco). KRON, 1984-. Founded "Neighborhood Weather" reports, live from various Bay Area locales, to dramatize variety in San Francisco weather. KMGH (Denver), early 1980s; also WKBW, Buffalo. Graduate of Colgate University.

VOLKMAN, Harry (Chicago). Pioneer in professional weathercasting. WBBM, 1978-; WGN, 1974-78, 1967-70; WMAQ, 1970-74, 1959-67. Also, KOTV (Tulsa), 1950-52; WKY (now KTVY, Oklahoma City), 1952-55; KWTV (Oklahoma City), 1955-59. Broadcast first televised tornado warning in United States, 1952. Received Chicago Emmy awards in 1962, 1965, 1968. Studied physics and mathematics, Tufts College; meteorology, Spartan School of Aeronautics, Tulsa; radio and television, University of Oklahoma. 1981 AMS Meteorologist of the Year; past chairman, Board of Radio and Television Weathercasters.

VOSS, Valerie (National). First female meteorologist-weathercaster on national television. Began at WITI (Milwaukee), in 1979; weather anchor for "Morning," CBS, March-October 1980. Also at WABC (New York), 1981; Satellite News Network, 1982-83; WRC (Washington), 1983-84; WTVN (Columbus), 1984-85. Morning weathercaster on Cable News Network, 1986-. B.S. in meteorology, Northern Illinois University. AMS seal; served as chairman, AMS Board of Broadcast Meteorology.

WILLIAMS, Jim (Oklahoma City). KTVY, 1958-. Aviation meteorologist, 1956-58; Air Force meteorology instructor, 1952-56. B.A. in geography/meteorology, Oklahoma State University. AMS sealholder; 1986 AMS Award for Outstanding Service by a Broadcast Meteorologist.

WINTERLING, George (Jacksonville). Pioneer in weather map animation and hurricane coverage. WJXT, 1962-. Air Force meteorologist and NWS forecaster, 1950s. B.S. in meteorology, Florida State University. AMS Fellow; Outstanding Service by a Broadcast Meteorologist, 1984.

WITTE, Joe (National, Philadelphia, New York, Seattle). "NBC News at Sunrise" and occasional appearances on "Today," 1983-. Also, WITI (Milwaukee), 1981-83; WABC (New York), 1980-81; KYW (Philadelphia),

Joe Witte ("NBC News at Sunrise"). (Courtesy NBC)

1978–80; WCBS (New York), 1974–78; KING (Seattle), 1970–74. Created several weather-graphic tools. Government researcher on Mt. Rainier and Mt. Olympus, Washington, 1960s. Organized United States telephone hotline for public inquiries on hurricanes. B.S., M.S. in meteorology, University of Washington. AMS sealholder.

WOODS, Don (Tulsa). Longtime artist-weathercaster. KTUL, 1954–89. Navy meteorologist, 1940s; National Weather Service, 1948–53. Created Gusty, a trademarked character used on each Woods weathercast and displayed at the Smithsonian Institution. AMS sealholder.

YOCKEY, Marcia (Evansville, Indiana). One of the longest-serving female weathercasters. WFIE, 1971–88, 1953–57; WTVW, 1957–71. Weather Bureau meteorologist, 1944–53. Avid pilot. Studied chemistry, Evansville College.

YOULE, John Clinton (Chicago, National). First network weathercaster. Trained as Air Force meteorologist during World War II. Writer-editor for NBC in Chicago in late 1940s. Regular on "Camel News Caravan," NBC, 1949–59, with reports from one to three times weekly. Also did local weather on WNBQ, Chicago, in 1950s. Retired from weathercasting in 1960s for business endeavors; served one term in the Illinois legislature.

Appendix II: American Meteorological Society Awards

As a supporter of quality weather programs on radio and television, the American Meteorological Society (AMS) has sponsored weathercaster awards for some 30 years. Below, courtesy of the AMS, these citations have been reprinted from the *Bulletin of the American Meteorological Society* (August 1988), including a list of all AMS awards given to television or radio stations, weathercasters, or companies that support weathercasting.

The Award for Outstanding Service by a Broadcast Meteorologist

1977   **Roy L. Leep, Jr.,** "for outstanding leadership and innovations in weathercasting which bring great credit to him and distinction to the Society and the profession, and for setting high standards for all broadcast meteorologists."

1980   **Donald E. Kent,** "for his pioneering and continuing efforts in demonstrating that there is a vast and enthusiastic audience for a knowledgeable, in-depth treatment of weather facts and forecasts."

1981   **Conrad L. Johnson,** "for his outstanding leadership in weathercasting, which brings great credit and distinction to the Society and the profession; also for setting high standards for all broadcast meteorology."

1982   **Harry A. Volkman,** "for outstanding service to his community and the meteorological profession for the past quarter century, and for his work in furthering public education in meteorology in the Chicago area."

1983   **John S. Coleman,** "for his many years of service in presenting weather reports of high informational, educational and professional quality to a national television audience, and for his pioneering efforts in establishing a national cable weather channel combining the latest advances in broadcast technology, weather science, and meteorological communications."

1984   **George A. Winterling,** "for his skills and pioneering efforts in developing animated weather presentations that allow the viewer to better understand the world of meteorology, and for continued excellence and high standards employed in his weather broadcasts."

1985   **Gregory B. Fishel** and **William Schmidt,** "for outstanding service to WRAL-TV viewers and area radio listeners in connection with the tornado outbreak of March 28, 1984, and for assistance to the National Weather Service in relaying warnings after the NOAA Weather Wire was disabled."

1986   **James D. Williams,** "for twenty-eight years of outstanding broadcast weather service to television viewers of central Oklahoma and for pioneering achievements in media presentation of weather radar data."

1987   **Richard R. Fletcher,** "for outstanding service to viewers during the hurricane season of 1985."

1988   **Raymond E. Falconer,** "for tens of thousands of competent and congenial radio weather forecasts and for decades of public education about the atmosphere."

The Award for Outstanding Services to Meteorology by a Corporation

1954   **National Broadcasting System,** "for performing an important public service through television coverage of the weather on its network programs, 'Today' with Dave Garroway and James Clayton Fidler and 'News Caravan' with John Cameron Swayze and John Clinton Youle."

1957   **The Travelers Insurance Companies,** "for their foresight, initiative, and courage in promoting and developing an entirely new field of specialized weather service for the American public."

1970   **A. H. Glenn & Associates, Murray and Trettel, Inc., North American Weather Consultants, Northeast Weather Service,** and **Weather Corporation of America.** Each was cited for "its pioneering the practice of private meteorology in the United States, thereby helping to develop an industry which has made significant contributions to the American economy."

1973   **WTVT Television Service** of Tampa, Fla., "for outstanding performance in providing full coverage on television and through its own publications promoting meteorology, meteorological organizations, and support for weather activities by the public sector."

1982   **Maryland Center for Public Broadcasting,** "for its major contribution to both aviation safety and public education in meteorology over the past decade, by providing timely, informative, and educational weather information first on *Aviation Weather* and since 1978 on *A.M. Weather,* a program of extraordinary professional merit now being aired by over 250 Public Broadcasting Service stations nationwide."

Special Awards and Citations

1957   **Radio Station KSOK** of Arkansas City, Kansas, "for its action in initiating a telephone call to the Weather Bureau Office in Wichita reporting that information has been received on tornadic activity near Maple City and Otto, Kansas. The tornado warning issued by the Wichita Office as a result of this call is believed to have saved the lives of at least six persons, possibly more."

Television Station WKY-TV of Oklahoma City, Okla., "for their enthusiastic support of meteorology in their area. With a professional meteorologist serving as Publicity Director and Meteorologist for WKY-TV, the weather programs are found to be most interesting and emphasize progress made in meteorology. WKY-TV was also instrumental, several years back, in securing the reproduction rights to the now famous Corn Tornado movie film which they then made available to training agencies at cost."

1969   **Station KICD,** Spencer, Iowa, "in recognition of its public service in broadcasting during the period of severe weather over northwest Iowa on June 13, 1968, advisories which were instrumental in saving lives."

1970   **WMAQ-TV,** Chicago, Ill., "for outstanding public service in disseminating timely weather information particularly on severe storms."

1971   **National Broadcasting Company,** "for its 'Today' television program for the excellent presentation of meteorological information which educates the public on the nature of weather and the importance of protecting the public against its hazards."

      WKY Television System, Incorporated, of Oklahoma City, "for its sense of public responsibility in making available to the National Severe Storms Laboratory its transmitter tower for the study of the atmospheric layer near the ground."

1973   **James W. Reid,** posthumously, "for originating and producing the program 'How's the Weather' in the TN Radio Network for over thirty years and for his efforts in organizing the North Carolina Chapter of the American Meteorological Society."

1976   **Albert W. Duckworth,** "for his oustanding service to the people of Southern Louisiana by his untiring and knowledgeable coverage on WWL Radio and Television during the threat of Hurricane Carmen in September 1974."

1977   **John F. Henz** and **Vincent R. Scheetz,** "for an outstanding example of the use of meteorological knowledge and radio in the public interest during the flash flood situation in the Big Thompson Canyon of Colorado on July 31 and August 1, 1976."

      Radio Station KCOL, Ft. Collins, Colo., "for an outstanding example of emergency programming to ensure prompt radio dissemination of critical meteorological information in the public interest during the flash flood situation in the Big Thompson Canyon of Colorado on July 31 and August 1, 1976."

**Holders of the AMS Seal of Approval for Television
(Listed by Certificate Number)**

*Deceased
**Inactive

1	Francis K. Davis, Jr.	Honorary	January	1959
2	Kenneth H. Jehn*	Honorary	January	1959
3	Henry W. Kinnan	Honorary	January	1959
4	Milton F. Barlow**		January	1960
5	Warren A. Culbertson**		January	1960
6	Bob Thomas**		January	1960
7	Robert L. Hendrick**		January	1960
8	Charles Hosler		January	1960
9	George M. Howe**		January	1960
10	Roy L. Leep		January	1960
11	James M. Macdonald, Jr.**		January	1960
12	Frederick P. Ostby, Jr.**		January	1960
13	Donald E. Kent**		January	1960
14	Peter M. Kuhn**		January	1960
15	Milton A. Strauss**		January	1960
16	Gordon B. Weir*		January	1960
17	Joe Hines Wolters**		January	1960
18	Cecil C. Carrier**		January	1960
19	John C. Capell**		April	1960
20	Robert C. Copeland		April	1960
21	D. Clay McDowell		April	1960
22	Albert E. Boyer, Jr.**		October	1960
23	Harry A. Volkman		October	1960
24	Howard M. Frazier**		October	1960
25	H. Dale Milford		November	1960
26	Frank H. Forrester**		November	1960
27	Leon M. Rottman		December	1960
28	James C. Fidler	Honorary	January	1961
29	William Crawford*		April	1961
30	Joseph W. Denardo		April	1961
31	Verl D. Dotson**		April	1961
32	Charles F. Thomas**		August	1961
33	Nash C. Roberts, Jr.**		November	1961
34	Howard E. Reiquam**		November	1961
35	Norman J. MacDonald**		January	1962
36	Harry C. Zimmerman**		February	1962
37	Norman K. Wagner**		May	1962

38	Robert E. Amsberry**	May	1962
39	Robert E. Lynott**	June	1962
40	Howard H. Hanks, Jr.*	June	1962
41	Roland R. Kessler**	June	1962
42	George A. Winterling	May	1963
43	Loren F. Boatman	July	1963
44	James E. Smith	November	1963
45	Richard D. Goddard	July	1964
46	Charles W. Stump*	July	1964
47	Albert W. Duckworth**	September	1964
48	Clifford H. Watkins**	March	1965
49	Hubert D. Bagley**	March	1965
50	George W. Sickels, Jr.**	May	1965
51	John W. Hambleton**	July	1966
52	Frank Field	July	1966
53	David C. Guild	September	1966
54	Seth D. Kemble**	February	1967
55	Conrad L. Johnson**	April	1967
56	Horace W. Meredith**	May	1967
57	Leonard M. Slesick	May	1967
58	Robert F. Zames**	May	1967
59	Frederick J. Norman**	September	1967
60	W. Paul Catoe**	September	1967
61	John H. Cromwell**	March	1968
62	James D. Williams**	April	1968
63	Ronald L. Godbey**	September	1968
64	Arthur C. Roberts**	September	1968
65	Boyd E. Quate**	September	1968
66	Tony Sands**	February	1969
67	Robert Weaver	July	1969
68	Jehu D. Ashmore**	August	1969
69	Robert Kudzma**	August	1969
70	Charles Melvin Gertz	October	1969
71	Robert E. Wademan**	October	1969
72	Joel N. Myers**	October	1969
73	John J. Cahir**	October	1969
74	John T. Ghiorse, Jr.	October	1969
75	Richard G. Andrews**	October	1969
76	Charles M. Umpenhour	December	1969
77	William N. Seiler**	July	1970
78	George R. Wooten, Jr.**	September	1970
79	Robert T. Ryan	January	1971
80	Thomas G. Wills	May	1971

81	Roger L. Triemstra	May	1971
82	Elliot Abrams**	May	1971
83	Sidney O. Barnard**	July	1971
84	William M. Zeliff	July	1971
85	Paul S. Joseph	July	1971
86	Charles Middleton**	July	1971
87	Douglas B. Cargill**	October	1971
88	Harry J. Green**	November	1971
89	Mark E. Eubank	March	1972
90	Robert E. Zabrecky	March	1972
91	William S. Thorpe**	March	1972
92	George R. Fischbeck**	May	1972
93	John T. McMurray**	September	1972
94	H. Joe Witte**	November	1972
95	Wayne G. Winston	December	1972
96	June Bacon-Bercey**	December	1972
97	Walton W. Jones	December	1972
98	Walter A. Lyons	December	1972
99	Eric A. Meindl**	December	1972
100	John F. Beckman	April	1973
101	Thomas J. Mahoney	October	1973
102	Mark H. Schumacher**	October	1973
103	Joseph P. Sobel	October	1973
104	Allen H. Motew**	October	1973
105	Virginia J. Bigler-Engler**	December	1973
106	Jym R. Ganahl	December	1973
107	Ross J. Dixon, Jr.**	April	1974
108	William B. Hovey**	April	1974
109	John A. Ebert**	March	1974
110	Patrick B. Moore**	May	1974
111	Allan C. Eustis	July	1974
112	Richard E. Albert	July	1974
113	Craig J. Woods	July	1974
114	Winston H. Jervis, Jr.**	July	1974
115	James J. O'Donnell	July	1974
116	William R. Kowal	July	1974
117	Norman C. Taylor	July	1974
118	Russell G. DuBuc**	January	1975
119	Thomas E. Skilling, III	January	1975
120	Fred W. Weiss	January	1975
121	Robert D. Welti**	January	1975
122	Russell F. Minshew	January	1975
123	Ronald L. Howes	March	1975

124	Norman F. Lewis	April	1975
125	John F. Chandik	April	1975
126	Kenneth R. Rainey**	April	1975
127	John R. Bradshaw**	May	1975
128	Peter F. Giddings	June	1975
129	Terence F. Kelly	July	1975
130	Michael R. Smith	August	1975
131	Dennis W. Feltgen	October	1975
132	Cecil S. Keen**	January	1976
133	Kenneth B. McCool**	April	1976
134	John B. Walls**	April	1976
135	Alan S. Mitleider**	April	1976
136	David S. Marsh	April	1976
137	Paul E. Barys	July	1976
138	James F. Pass**	July	1976
139	Raymond L. Boylan	January	1977
140	Joel P. Bartlett, Jr.	January	1977
141	Robert J. Roseman**	January	1977
142	Donald S. Noe**	November	1977
143	Richard D. McLaughlin**	November	1977
144	Don R. Westbrook	January	1978
145	Charles E. Levy**	January	1978
146	Howard E. Shapiro**	January	1978
147	Valarie Ann Jones	January	1978
148	James Lee Menard**	January	1978
149	David P. Murray	January	1978
150	Donald K. Woods	April	1978
151	Richard W. Faurot	April	1978
152	Jimmie D. Giles	April	1978
153	Richard J. Katz**	April	1978
154	Gerald A. Hodak	July	1978
155	Gary Shore	July	1978
156	Roy Fred Finden	July	1978
157	Richard J. Mancini**	July	1978
158	Gordon D. Rasmussen	July	1978
159	Fred J. Jenkins**	July	1978
160	Richard R. Fletcher	July	1978
161	Vincent M. Miller**	July	1978
162	Craig A. Johnson	July	1978
163	James R. Little**	July	1978
164	Robert Paul Soper**	July	1978
165	Wayne M. Jenkins**	July	1978
166	Armin J. Ott	August	1978

167	Dale G. Noah**	August	1978
168	Jerome B. Taft, II	August	1978
169	Edward J. Ring**	August	1978
170	Theodore F. Fathauer	October	1978
171	Robert J. Kovachick	October	1978
172	Robert W. Jacobson, Jr.**	October	1978
173	Walter Cronise	October	1978
174	Michael D. Fairbourne	October	1978
175	Dallas D. Raines	October	1978
176	Mike A. Lozano, Jr.	October	1978
177	James M. Howl	March	1979
178	Paul S. Hagar	March	1979
179	William O. Eisenhood	March	1979
180	Robert L. O'Wril*	March	1979
181	H. Michael Mogil**	April	1979
182	Robert W. Dixon	April	1979
183	Leonard R. Elfervig	April	1979
184	Patrick M. Prokop	April	1979
185	Paul W. Cousins	April	1979
186	Richard C. Przywarty**	April	1979
187	Dan J. True	April	1979
188	Merril D. Teller	April	1979
189	Bruce W. Schwoegler	April	1979
190	Jeffrey P. Walker**	April	1979
191	Richard R. Warren**	July	1979
192	F. Calvin Sisto	July	1979
193	William Dale Peterson	July	1979
194	Jeffrey B. Gallant**	September	1979
195	Keith Eichner**	September	1979
196	Robert W. McLain	October	1979
197	William D. Kamal	October	1979
198	Michael H. Graham	November	1979
199	Arthur E. Hornberger, Jr.**	November	1979
200	Daniel D. Maly	November	1979
201	Warren D. Nolan	November	1979
202	Dale N. Zunke	November	1979
203	Daniel M. Atkinson, Jr.	March	1980
204	Barry M. Burbank	March	1980
205	David I. Duisik	March	1980
206	Mark S. Russell**	March	1980
207	C. Michael Rucker	April	1980
208	Kurt R. Schmitz	May	1980
209	Harry V. Wappler	July	1980

210	Paul G. Knight	December	1980
211	Michael G. Reeves	December	1980
212	Robert L. Schwartz	December	1980
213	William H. Schubert	December	1980
214	Wayne C. Shattuck	December	1980
215	Dennis L. Smith	December	1980
216	Benjamin D. Gelber	March	1981
217	Todd Gross	March	1981
218	Kenneth T. Koch	March	1981
219	John J. Malan	March	1981
220	Jack M. Mercer	March	1981
221	Glenn E. Schwartz	March	1981
222	Stanley J. Stachak	March	1981
223	Joseph A. Dandrea	April	1981
224	Thomas L. Magnuson	April	1981
225	Joseph C. Conway	June	1981
226	Brian S. Norcross	June	1981
227	Roberta Ann Marshment	June	1981
228	Harvey Leonard	August	1981
229	James L. Madaus	August	1981
230	Lawrence J. Mulholland**	August	1981
231	James H. Reif	August	1981
232	John Robert Willing	August	1981
233	William H. Annen	September	1981
234	John D. Flanders**	September	1981
235	James Brian Flowers	September	1981
236	Kevin M. O'Connell	September	1981
237	Ronald W. Jackson	October	1981
238	Albert L. Roker	November	1981
239	James W. Bosley, Sr.	December	1981
240	Wayne P. Chandler**	December	1981
241	Daniel G. Dobrowolski	December	1981
242	Robert E. Gregory	December	1981
243	Thomas Loffman	January	1982
244	Nancy A. Russo Chapman**	January	1982
245	Timothy A. Chuey	March	1982
246	Dennis G. Frary	March	1982
247	Neil E. Kastor	March	1982
248	Donald T. McNeely	March	1982
249	Michael P. Nelson	March	1982
250	Donald O. Novak	March	1982
251	Eugene M. Rubin	March	1982
252	Jocelyn K. White**	May	1982

253	Carey L. Kinsey, Jr.	May	1982
254	David K. Towne	June	1982
255	Richard A. Addis	June	1982
256	Lawrence D. Hill	June	1982
257	James G. Duncan	June	1982
258	Vincent D. Condella, Jr.	June	1982
259	Glenn Noel Burns	June	1982
260	Louis K. McNally, III**	June	1982
261	Douglas P. Kruhoeffer	June	1982
262	Robert Becker	August	1982
263	Stuart M. Bowersox	August	1982
264	Gregory B. Fishel	August	1982
265	Anthony O'Leary Johnson	August	1982
266	Mark L. Nichols**	August	1982
267	Neal B. Pascal	August	1982
268	Donald J. Paul	August	1982
269	Barry A. Richwien	August	1982
270	Carl E. Weiss, Jr.	August	1982
271	Glenn C. Wood	August	1982
272	Ronald A. Yaros	August	1982
273	Not included in AMS listings.		
274	John G. Bernier	September	1982
275	Clifford M. Nicholson	September	1982
276	William E. Kuster	September	1982
277	Frank B. Deal, Jr.	September	1982
278	John James Collins	September	1982
279	John J. Campbell**	September	1982
280	Thomas E. Hale	September	1982
281	Robert O. Baron	September	1982
282	David W. Dahl	September	1982
283	Willis Bryan Owings	September	1982
284	Daniel L. Milham	September	1982
285	Malcolm P. Sillars	September	1982
286	Andre Marc Bernier	January	1983
287	John T. Bielski	January	1983
288	Edward A. Duranczyk, Jr.	January	1983
289	William C. Keneely**	January	1983
290	Michael V. Modrick**	January	1983
291	Cyril E. Nefstead	January	1983
292	Leon F. Pettersen	January	1983
293	James J. Schnebelt	January	1983
294	Mark R. Koontz	January	1983
295	Donald W. Carson	March	1983

296	David S. Eiser	March	1983
297	Mark Mancuso	March	1983
298	Randall D. Ollis	March	1983
299	Thomas C. Rector	March	1983
300	Terry L. Swails	March	1983
301	Nicholas J. Gregory	March	1983
302	Chuck F. Wiese**	March	1983
303	Barton J. Adrian	March	1983
304	Raymond J. Ban	March	1983
305	Christopher T. Hohmann	March	1983
306	Gary W. Ley	March	1983
307	Albert M. Bolton	May	1983
308	Jim F. Riggs	May	1983
309	Tim Ross	June	1983
310	Donald C. Buser	June	1983
311	Miles S. Muzio	June	1983
312	Phil Whitelaw	June	1983
313	Jeffrey F. Kronschnabel	July	1983
314	Anthony Cavalier	July	1983
315	Dale Alan Dockus	July	1983
316	David N. Eichorn	August	1983
317	John M. Wendel	August	1983
318	John C. Dooley	August	1983
319	Sally P. Schmies	August	1983
320	Michael L. Thompson	September	1983
321	Steven W. Browne	September	1983
322	Steven L. Horstmeyer	September	1983
323	Stephen M. Letro**	September	1983
324	David J. Relihan	September	1983
325	Paul J. Silvestri	September	1983
326	Storm E. Field	October	1983
327	James E. Brihan	October	1983
328	Karen Anne Filloon	October	1983
329	Timothy W. Deegan	November	1983
330	Henry B. Pringle	November	1983
331	Jonathan Davies	November	1983
332	Robert Arnold**	November	1983
333	Donald L. Edwards**	November	1983
334	Bradford A. Field	December	1983
335	Valerie Voss Collins	December	1983
336	John C. Fischer	February	1984
337	Gail J. Brodhead	February	1984
338	Joseph J. Calhoun	June	1984

339	Joseph Cioffi	June	1984
340	Kevin D. Williams	June	1984
341	David T. Lawyer	August	1984
342	Chris D. Thompson	August	1984
343	Charles S. Herring	September	1984
344	Troy M. Kimmel, Jr.	September	1984
345	Jeffrey B. Lawson	September	1984
346	Donald K. Chilo**	September	1984
347	Lorraine Stinnett	September	1984
348	William G. Reh	September	1984
349	David C. Carlson	December	1984
350	Paul H. Gross	December	1984
351	Jeffrey M. Heaton	December	1984
352	Brian D. Davis	December	1984
353	David P. Barnes, Jr.	February	1985
354	David H. Brown	February	1985
355	Michael H. McClellan	February	1985
356	John R. Hope	February	1985
357	Michael J. Hoffman	February	1985
358	Robert E. Day, Jr.	February	1985
359	Rufus R. Hafer**	February	1985
360	Ron Allen	February	1985
361	Robert J. Hocks	February	1985
362	David A. Oliver	February	1985
363	Joseph A. Pietrowicz**	March	1985
364	John A. Fuller	March	1985
365	Rebecca Ellen Erwin	March	1985
366	James P. Roemer**	March	1985
367	Nicholas D. Schordje	March	1985
368	Edward W. Pearl	May	1985
369	James T. Gandy	June	1985
370	Mario J. Gomez	June	1985
371	Daniel Riley Bowman	June	1985
372	Greg Paul Bostwick	June	1985
373	Dennis John Hodges	June	1985
374	Eric T. DeZubay	June	1985
375	Paul J. Mroz	June	1985
376	Matthew Zaffino	June	1985
377	Janice Wages Huff	July	1985
378	Richard K. Griffin	July	1985
379	Stephen R. Newman	July	1985
380	Danny E. Satterfield	July	1985
381	Norman C. Sebastian	July	1985

382	Thomas J. Kierein	September	1985
383	George D. Lessens	September	1985
384	Joseph Lizura	September	1985
385	Royal L. Norman, Jr.	September	1985
386	Duane D. Harding	October	1985
387	Michael G. Cejka	October	1985
388	Jay Lennartson	October	1985
390	Steven P. Caporizzo	October	1985
391	William H. Evans	October	1985
392	Wayne G. Mahar	October	1985
393	Arnold Rosen	October	1985
394	Herbert Eugene Stevens	October	1985
395	David M. Miller	October	1985
396	Wayne Carr Hartung	November	1985
397	Robert G. Lindmeier	November	1985
398	Daniel W. McCarthy**	December	1985
399	Thaddeus J. Maguire	December	1985
400	Andrew L. Weingarten	December	1985
401	Robert C. Brough	December	1985
402	Chris S. Edwards	January	1986
403	Kenneth A. Schulz	January	1986
404	Brian A. Albrecht	February	1986
405	Michael Bono	February	1986
406	James R. Clarke	February	1986
407	Andrew A. Avalos	March	1986
408	Ted William Keller, Jr.	March	1986
409	Philip S. Schwarz	March	1986
410	John Warren Adams	March	1986
411	James Robert Wegner	March	1986
412	William J. Steffen	April	1986
413	Lana Cheryl Jones	April	1986
414	Sharon L. Graves	May	1986
415	Shane Richard Hollett	May	1986
416	Donald F. Morelli	May	1986
417	David A. Carmichael	June	1986
418	David C. Whitford	June	1986
419	Alan S. Winfield	July	1986
420	John M. Wooldridge	July	1986
421	David S. Huntress	August	1986
422	Tom Lilley (Non-member)	August	1986
423	John G. Waunsch	September	1986
424	Matthew P. Belau	October	1986
425	Bryan T. Busby	October	1986

426	Bruce E. Kalinowski	October	1986
427	Ronald G. Penzkowski	October	1986
428	Mark B. Rosenthal**	October	1986
429	Sharon Louise Akemann**	November	1986
430	Thomas M. Tasselmyer	December	1986
431	George S. Zabrecky	December	1986
432	Byron K. Webre	February	1987
433	Bruce J. Deprest	February	1987
434	Holice H. Kaderli, Jr.	February	1987
435	Glenn E. Johnson	February	1987
436	Elmer M. Childress	March	1987
437	Thomas J. Bevacqua	April	1987
438	Robert W. Cameron**	April	1987
439	Keith Charles Westerlage	April	1987
440	James F. Stewart	April	1987
441	Andrew C. Provenzano	April	1987
442	Michael S. Rampy**	April	1987
443	John Charles Gaughan, Jr.	April	1987
444	Gordon R. Behm	May	1987
445	Jeffrey T. Jensen	May	1987
446	William S. Schmidt**	May	1987
447	Tom Burse	May	1987
448	Brian H. Durst	May	1987
449	Martha Lynn Austin	June	1987
450	Bradford T. Huffines	October	1987
451	Rene J. Brunet, III	October	1987
452	Richard A. Woodford	October	1987
453	Robert W. Demers	October	1987
454	Craig S. Schellsmidt	October	1987
455	Paul O. G. Heppner	October	1987
456	John R. Boston**	October	1987
457	John A. Cessarich**	October	1987
458	Theodore E. Textor	November	1987
459	Daryl W. McCollister	December	1987
460	Brian T. Alworth	December	1987
461	Victoria Lee Griffin	December	1987
462	Steven R. Cascione	December	1987
463	Kenneth A. Aucoin	December	1987
464	John G. Fausett	December	1987
465	David R. Hartman	December	1987
466	William E. Randby**	December	1987
467	Frederick G. Rixe	December	1987
468	Philip G. Schreck	December	1987

469	Martin E. Coniglio	January	1988
470	James M. Corbin, III	January	1988
471	Steve C. LaNore	January	1988
472	Daniel W. Pope	January	1988
473	David L. Schaffer	January	1988
474	James M. Cantore	January	1988
475	Jeffrey D. Klotz	January	1988
476	Steven C. Bray	February	1988
477	Declan P. Cannon	February	1988
478	Frank J. Cariello	February	1988
479	Patricia Lynn Cooper	February	1988
480	Christopher R. Grote	February	1988
481	Jon D. Loufman	February	1988
482	Michael J. Madson	February	1988
483	Frank J. Marsik	February	1988
484	Darlene A. Periconi	February	1988
485	Phillip P. Stanley	February	1988
486	Alan R. Sealls	February	1988
487	Suzanne D. Sill	February	1988
488	Jeffrey B. Renner	February	1988
489	Paul N. Dellegatto	March	1988
490	David G. Dierks	March	1988
491	Mark L. Evangelista	March	1988
492	James W. Jaggers	March	1988
493	Ronald A. Hearst, II	March	1988
494	Noreen Roberts Clark	April	1988
495	Thomas N. Clark	April	1988
496	Alan L. Mitchell	April	1988
497	Robert F. Riggio	April	1988
498	Charles T. Shutt	April	1988
499	Tamara A. Miller-Glahn	May	1988
500	George G. Brown	May	1988
501	Robert H. Rosenzweig	May	1988
502	Heidi E. Sonen	June	1988
503	Jeffrey G. Latham	June	1988

Notes

Many of the references below coincide with entries in the Bibliography that serve as especially useful materials on weathercasting. All such references are given below in their entirety on first use. BAMS denotes the *Bulletin of the American Meteorological Society.*

Chapter 1. "And Now, the Forecast..."

1. David Shaw, "Weather: Everyone's No. 1 Story," *Los Angeles Times,* 1 Mar. 1981, 1.
2. National Oceanic and Atmospheric Administration, *Radio and Television Dissemination Issue Study,* May 1981 (radio-television file, Office of Constituent Affairs, National Weather Service, Silver Spring, Maryland), 10.
3. "Weathercasters Shine News in Survey," *Television/Radio Age,* 16 Sept. 1985, 48.
4. Jerry Adler, "A Case of Morning Sickness," *Newsweek,* 13 Mar. 1989, 61.
5. "Fair and Wet," *TV Guide,* 4 Feb. 1956, 12.
6. Glenn Garelik, "The Weather Peddlers," *Discover* (April 1985): 24.
7. Patrick Hughes, *American Weather Stories* (Washington: U.S. Department of Commerce, 1976), 26.
8. Joseph Frank, *The Beginnings of the English Newspaper, 1620-1660* (Cambridge: Harvard Univ., 1961), 227.
9. Lucy Brown, *Victorian News and Newspapers* (Oxford: Clarendon Press, 1985), 253-54.
10. Edwin Emery and Michael Emery, *The Press and America,* 4th ed. (Englewood Cliffs, N.J.: Prentice-Hall, 1978, 119.
11. Emery and Emery, *The Press and America,* 222.
12. A. B. C. Whipple, *Storm* (Alexandria, Va.: Time-Life Books, 1982), 77.
13. James C. Fidler, "Popularizing the Weather Broadcast," BAMS 19 (1938): 312-13.
14. "Mary Had One and So Did We," *New York Daily News,* 12 July 1981, 5.
15. Cobbett Steinberg, *TV Facts* (New York: Facts on File Publications, 1985), 85.
16. Steinberg, *TV Facts,* 401.

17. Mitchell Charnley, *News by Radio* (New York: Macmillan, 1948), 253–54.

18. "Louis Allen: Forecasting's Vicissitudes," *Washington Star,* 9 Mar. 1976, A1.

19. "Louis Allen, WTOP Weather Newsman," *Washington Post,* 10 May 1976, B6.

20. John Clinton Youle, phone interview, 3 Jan. 1989.

21. Transcribed from videotape, "Camel News Caravan," 30 Dec. 1949, viewed at U.S. Library of Congress, Washington, 28 Feb. 1989.

22. Eugene Dodson, "The Professional Broadcast Meteorologist as Seen by Management," BAMS 49 (1968): 366–67.

23. Steinberg, *TV Facts,* 85.

24. Steinberg, *TV Facts,* 401.

25. "Tricky Weather," *Newsweek,* 22 Apr. 1957, 72.

26. Gilbert Seldes, "Weather Reports (Review)," *TV Guide,* 3 Mar. 1963, 5.

27. K. H. Jehn, "Recognition of Competence in Weathercasting: The AMS Seal of Approval Program," BAMS 40 (1959): 85.

28. Francis Davis, "Weather Is No Laughing Matter," *TV Guide,* 23 July 1955, 10.

29. "Tricky Weather," 72.

30. Jehn, "Recognition," 86–88.

31. Jehn, "Radio and Television Weathercasting — The Seal of Approval Program after Five Years," BAMS 45 (1964): 491–92.

32. "An Improvement in TV Weather Forecasts," *TV Guide,* 18 July 1959, inside front cover.

33. Dave Murray, phone interview, 12 Feb. 1989.

34. Lance Morrow, "The Wonderful Art of Weathercasting," *Time,* 17 Mar. 1980, 61.

Chapter 2. Weathercasting Today

1. *The World Alamanac and Books of Facts* (New York: Pharos Books, 1989), 356.

2. Bill Wagner, "When Weather Is the Lead," *RTNDA Communicator* (Dec. 1985): 9.

3. Melvin Durslag, "TV Weathermen," *TV Guide,* 24 Mar. 1973, 9.

4. Richard F. Shepard, "TV Notes: Role of Weathercasters," *New York Times,* 1 Mar. 1984, C22.

5. "Eliminating the Weatherman," *TV Guide,* 9 Apr. 1977, A4.

6. Dave Murray, phone interview, 12 Feb. 1989.

7. Neil Frank, phone interview, 26 Jan. 1989.

8. "Seal of Approval Program," BAMS 63 (1982): 914.

9. "Seal of Approval Program," 914.

10. "The Radio and Television Seal of Approval Program of the Society: Policies and Procedures," BAMS 64 (1983): 11.

11. Kerry D. Teverbaugh and John G. Bernier, "Purposes of the National Weather Association Committee on Television and Radio Weathercasting," *National Weather Digest* 7 (Feb. 1982): 5–6.

12. "Weathercaster Certification," *National Weather Digest* 9 (Aug. 1984): 8.

13. Willard Scott, *The Joy of Living* (New York: Coward, McCann and Geoghegan, 1982), 141–51.

14. "The Wind Rose," *American Weather Observer* (Oct. 1988): 14.)

15. "Wind Rose," 14.

16. "The Markets Ranked by Size," *Broadcasting Cablecasting Yearbook 1988* (Washington: Broadcasting Publications, 1989), C217–20.

17. Information and quotes in this section are from a personal interview with Bob Ryan at WRC-TV, Washington, 27 Feb. 1989.

18. Information and quotes in this section are from a personal interview with Harry Spohn at KNOP, North Platte, 10 June 1989.

19. Harry Spohn, phone interview, 31 July 1989.

Chapter 3. From Silly to Serious

1. Fidler, "Popularizing the Weather," 313.

2. Fidler, "Weather Via Television," BAMS 29 (1948): 330.

3. Francis Davis, "The Role of the Meteorologist in Radio and Television," BAMS 29 (1948): 516.

4. R. G. Stone, "The Weatherman Eyes Television," BAMS 30 (1949): 34.

5. Stone, "Weatherman," 34–35.

6. Stone, "Weatherman," 34.

7. "Fair-Weather Friends," *Time,* 12 Apr. 1968, 83.

8. Paul Joseph, phone interview, 22 March 1989.

9. "Weather Work for Women," *Life,* 28 Mar. 1955, 10.

10. "Tricky Weather," *Newsweek,* 22 Apr. 1957, 72.

11. Don Woods, phone interview, 12 Feb. 1989.

12. "America's Weather Wackies Take Their Forecasting with a Vane of Salt," *People,* 7 Sept. 1981, 27.

13. Shaw, "Everyone's No. 1 Story," 1.

14. Durslag, "TV Weathermen," 7.

15. Durslag, "TV Weathermen," 8.

16. Morrow, "Wonderful Art," 61.

17. "Willard Scott May Soon Feel Heat from a Frisky Competitor — Oregon's Bob the Weather Cat." *People,* 18 July 1988, 77.

18. "Weather Work," *Life,* 8.

19. Gerry Davis, *The Today Show: An Anecdotal History* (New York: William Morrow, 1987), 81–83.

20. "Morgus the Weather Ghoul," *TV Guide,* 21 Nov. 1959, 6–7.

21. Garelik, "Weather Peddlers," 29.

22. "Fair-Weather Friends," *Time,* 83.

23. Pam Proctor, "All They Do Is Talk About the Weather," *Parade,* 7 Sept. 1975, 13.

24. "Fair-Weather Friends," *Time,* 82.

25. Bob Ryan, interview, Washington, D.C., 27 Feb. 1989.

26. L. Michael Trapassc, Randy Bowman, and Laura Daniel, "TV Weather Forecasters," *RTNDA Communicator* (Dec. 1985): 17.

27. Marcia Yockey, phone interview, 10 July 1989.

28. Rebecca Reheis, phone interview, 22 Mar. 1989.

29. Howard Rosenberg, "It's Raining Television Weathermen/Comics!" *Los Angeles Times,* 8 July 1985, 6:8.

30. Durslag, "TV Weathermen," 7–8.

31. Durslag, "TV Weathermen," 8.

32. Garelik, "Weather Peddlers," 18.

33. Phil Foster, "The New England Weather Net," *Weatherwise* 12 (1959): 109–10.

34. Bud Kraeling, phone interview, 22 Mar. 1989.

35. Rosenberg, "Television Weathermen/Comics," 6:1.

36. Durslag, "TV Weathermen," 8.

37. Rebecca Reheis, phone interview, 22 Mar. 1989.

38. Shaw, "Everyone's No. 1 Story," 1.

39. Dennis Bowman, phone interview, 22 Mar. 1989.

Chapter 4. Television and the Weather Service

1. Roy Popkin, *The Environmental Science Services Administration* (New York: Praeger, 1967), 60.

2. John Baker, *Farm Broadcasting: The First 60 Years* (Ames: Iowa State Univ. Press, 1981), 18.

3. Baker, *Farm Broadcasting,* 18.

4. Bert Laverne Nelson, "The First Fifty Years of Weather Broadcasting," M.S. thesis, University of Utah, 1971, 2.

5. Edgar Calvert, "Radio Distribution of Forecasts and Warnings," BAMS 2 (1921): 74.

6. Baker, *Farm Broadcasting,* 18.

7. William Peck Banning, *Commercial Broadcasting Pioneer: The WEAF Experiment 1922–26* (Cambridge: Harvard Univ. Press, 1946), 85–86.

8. Baker, *Farm Broadcasting,* 18.

9. Fidler, "Popularizing the Weather Broadcast," 315.

10. Karl Compton, chair, *Report to the Secretary of Agriculture by the Committee on Relations Between the Weather Bureau and Private Forecasting Services* (Washington, D.C.: U.S. Department of Agriculture, 1940); radio-television file, NWS Office of Constituent Affairs, National Oceanic and Atmospheric Administration, Silver Spring, Md.

11. Fidler, "Popularizing the Weather Broadcast," 312.

12. Davis, "Role of the Meteorologist," 516.

13. Stone, "Weatherman Eyes Television," 35.

14. Frank Field, phone interview, 28 June 1989.

15. F. W. Reichelderfer to House Committee on Small Business, 4 May 1954; radio-television file, NWS Office of Constituent Affairs.

16. Complaint quoted by Carl Davis to Harold Corwin, 28 Apr. 1954; radio-television file, NWS Office of Constituent Affairs.

17. Reichelderfer to House Committee, 4 May 1954.

18. Reichelderfer to House Committee, 4 May 1954.

19. Paul Royster to Kenneth McClure, 29 June 1954; radio-television file, NWS Office of Constituent Affairs.

20. F. W. Reichelderfer, circular letter No. 27-54, 25 Aug. 1954; radio-television file, NWS Office of Constituent Affairs.

21. J. S. Myers to assistant, 21 Oct. 1954, radio-television file; NWS Office of Constituent Affairs.

22. *NOAA Directives Manual,* Department of Commerce, 16 Feb. 1971, Section 27-13.

23. Harry Feehan to Robert Carnahan, 3 Aug. 1972; radio-television file, NWS Office of Constituent Affairs.

24. Feehan to Carnahan, 3 Aug. 1972.

27. Robert Carnahan, background paper for radio-television policy study, 6 Jan. 1981; radio-television file, NWS Office of Constituent Affairs.

26. *NOAA Directives Manual,* 16 Jan. 1975, sec. 27-13.

27. *NOAA Directives Manual,* 1978.

28. *NOAA Directives Manual,* 16 Jan. 1975.

29. William Hallstead to Richard Frank, 24 Nov. 1978; radio-television file, NWS Office of Constituent Affairs.

30. Robert Carnahan, issue paper on "AM Weather," 24 July 1979; radio-television file, NWS Office of Constituent Affairs.

31. Richard Hallgren to NWS staff, 24 June 1981; radio-television file, NWS Office of Constituent Affairs.

32. Rodney J. Becker and Edward M. Gross, "National Weather Service Dissemination Systems," *RTNDA Communicator* (Dec. 1986): 11.

33. Patrick Hughes, *A Century of Weather Service* (New York: Gordon & Breach, 1970), 74.

34. "ESSA VHF Weather Radio Stations," *Weatherwise* 22 (1969): 157.

35. H. Michael Mogil and Herbert S. Groper, "NWS's Severe Local Storm Warning and Disaster Preparedness Programs," BAMS 58 (1977): 324-25.

36. Thomas J. Degregorio, "NOAA Weather Radio Needs Marketing!" *National Weather Digest* 12 (1987): 25.

37. Dennis McCarthy, "Warnings by Live, Simulated Broadcast from NOAA Weather Radio and Commercial Radio and Television," *National Weather Digest* 4 (1979): 8-9.

38. Degregorio, "NOAA Weather Radio," 25.

39. Lloyd A. Calhoun, "A Community TV Weather Service," *Weatherwise* 14 (1961): 245-47.

40. *Application of CATV to Public Weather Dissemination,* ESSA Technical Memorandum WBTM SR-43; radio-television file, NWS Office of Constituent Affairs.

41. Interim Report, Great Falls Cable TV Experiment, NWS Western Region, 1 Jan. 1974; radio-television file, NWS Office of Constituent Affairs, 1-3.

42. Interim Report, Great Falls Cable TV Experiment, 7-10.

43. *Radio and Television Dissemination Issue Study,* May 1981; radio-television file, NWS Office of Constituent Affairs, 14.

44. Mark Lorando, "Elena: An Exercise in Excess," *New Orleans Times-Picayune/States-Item,* 2 Sept. 1985, C-13.

45. Bob Levey, "In Oklahoma, He Weathers Well," *Washington Post,* 27 April 1985, A3.

46. Walter Gantz, "Redundancy and Accuracy of Television Station Weather Reports," *Journalism Quarterly* 59 (1982): 443-46.

Chapter 5. Technical Matters

1. Much of the information in this chapter was gleaned from personal knowledge and observation, and from literature distributed by the manufacturers of television-weather equipment.

2. Hugh Downs, *On Camera* (New York: G. P. Putnam's Sons, 1986), 137.

3. Donald R. Whitnaw, *A History of the United States Weather Bureau* (Urbana: Univ. of Illinois Press, 1961), 238.

4. George Winterling, phone interview, Aug. 1988.

5. Roy Leep, phone interview, Aug. 1988.

6. Frank Field, phone interview, 28 June 1989.

7. George Winterling, phone interview, Aug. 1988.

8. "The Society's Awards," BAMS 69 (1988): 915.

9. Douglas Merritt, *Television Graphics* (New York: Van Nostrand Reinhold, 1987), 44–45.

10. Whipple, *Storm,* 155–57.

11. Randy Bretz, *Techniques of Television Production,* 2d ed. (New York: McGraw-Hill, 1962), 281–82.

12. Shaw, "Everyone's No. 1 Story," 1; Gary England, personal interview, Oklahoma City, July 1986.

13. Eva Blinder, "Stations 'Eye' Storms with Doppler Radar," *Broadcast Management/Engineering* (Dec. 1985): 33.

14. Trapassc et al., "TV Weather Forecasters," 16.

Chapter 6 Diversifying the Weathercast

1. Barbara Matusow, *The Evening Stars* (Boston: Houghton Mifflin, 1983), 65.

2. Edward F. Taylor, "Joanne Simpson: Pathfinder for a Generation," *Weatherwise* 37 (1984): 182.

3. George Maksian, "Forecasters Can Vary Like the Weather," *New York Daily News,* 29 Apr. 1980, 70.

4. Davis, "Weather Is No Laughing Matter," 11.

5. Marcia Yockey, phone interview, 10 July 1989.

6. "Reliable Weathercasts," *Science News Letter* 69 (1956): 174.

7. Davis, "Weather Is No Laughing Matter," 11.

8. "Fair and Wet," *TV Guide,* 12.

9. "Tedi Thurman, Weathergirl Supreme," *TV Guide,* 19 Oct. 1957, 5–6.

10. "Weather Work for Women," *Life,* 8–9.

11. Gilbert Millstein, "The Weather Girls Ride Out a Storm," *New York Times Magazine,* 8 Oct. 1961, 64.

12. "An Improvement in TV Weather," *TV Guide,* inside front cover.

13. Shepard, "TV Notes," C22.

14. Marcia Yockey, phone interview, 10 July 1989.

15. Margaret A. LeMone and Patricia L. Waukau, "Women in Meteorology," BAMS 63 (1982): 1267.

16. June Bacon-Bercey, phone interview, 14 July 1989.

17. Durslag, "TV Weathermen," 6.

18. Proctor, "All They Do Is Talk," 13.

19. Valerie Voss, phone interview, 17 Feb. 1989.

20. Ibid.

21. Ray Ban, phone interview, 28 July 1989.

22. Rebecca Reheis, phone interview, 22 Mar. 1989.

23. Ibid.

24. Ibid.

25. Valerie Voss, phone interview, 17 Feb. 1989.

26. June Bacon-Bercey, "Is There a Future for Women Meteorologists in the Broadcast Field?"; paper delivered at the 12th Conference on Weathercasting of the American Meteorological Society, Seattle, 27 June 1982, 11.

27. Valerie Voss, phone interview, 17 Feb. 1989.

28. June Bacon-Bercey, phone interview, 14 July 1989.

29. Jim Tilmon, phone interview, 7 May 1989.

30. Maclovio Perez, phone interview, 12 Apr. 1989.

31. Garelik, "Weather Peddlers," 18.

32. Maclovio Perez, phone interview, 12 Apr. 1989.

33. June Bacon-Bercey, phone interview, 14 July 1989.

34. "Award for Outstanding Service by a Broadcast Meteorologist," BAMS 70 (1989): 652.

35. Jack Capell, phone interview, 28 June 1989.

36. Ibid.

37. Ibid.

38. Bob Lynott, *The Weather Tomorrow* (Portland, Oregon: Gadfly Press, 1987), 158.

39. Lynott, *Weather Tomorrow,* 157.

40. Jim Little, letter to author, 30 June 1988.

Chapter 7. Across the Nation

1. Allen Pearson and Frederick P. Otsby, Jr., "The Tornado Season of 1974," *Weatherwise* 28 (1975): 8.

2. Gerald Clarke, "Battle for the Morning," *Time,* 1 Dec. 1980, 62.

3. Davis, *Today Show,* 81.

4. Ibid.

5. William Gildea, "Weathermen: Putting a Freeze on Humor," *Washington Post,* 31 Jan. 1977, C1.

6. Harry F. Waters, "Morning Shows: ABC Tries Again," *Newsweek,* 17 Nov. 1975, 112.

7. John Coleman, phone interview, 28 June 1989.

8. Ibid.

9. Maksian, "Forecasters Can Vary," 70.

10. Ed Gross, phone interview, 14 July 1989.

11. *NOAA Directives Manual,* 16 Jan. 1975, sec. 27-13.

12. Cliff Naughton, "Pre-dawn Patrol," *Professional Pilot* (March 1988): 82–83.

13. Denice Walker, personal interview, Boulder, Colorado, 29 July 1989.

14. Steinberg, *TV Facts,* 89.

15. John Coleman, phone interview, 28 June 1989.

16. Leonard Ray Teel, "The Weather Channel," *Weatherwise* 35 (1982): 158–59.

17. Simon Appelbaum, "Second Wind," *CableVision,* 14 Nov. 1983, 44.

18. Appelbaum, "Second Wind," 38.

19. Appelbaum, "Second Wind," 39.

20. Ray Ban, phone interview, 21 July 1989.

21. Ibid.

22. Ibid.

23. Ibid.

Chapter 8. When Minutes Count

1. Popkin, *Environmental Science Services Administration,* 178–80.

2. "Radios from Arctic to Help American Business," BAMS 3 (1922): 90.

3. Popkin, *Environmental Science Services Administration,* 31.

4. Whipple, *Storm,* 19.

5. David Ludlum, *New England Weather Book* (Boston: Houghton Mifflin, 1976), 42.

6. Whipple, *Storm,* 25.

7. William Manchester, *The Glory and the Dream* (Boston: Little, Brown, 1975), 183.

8. Whipple, *Storm,* 109.

9. Robert Burpee, "Grady Norton: Hurricane Forecaster and Communicator," *Weather and Forecasting* 3 (1988): 249.

10. Whipple, *Storm,* 109.

11. Whitnaw, *History of the U.S. Weather Bureau,* 39–40.

12. *World Almanac 1989,* 525.

13. F. C. Bates, "Severe Local Storm Forecasts and Warnings and the General Public," BAMS 43 (1962): 288.

14. Nash Roberts, phone interview, 30 Jan. 1989.

15. Art Lake, phone interview, 7 July 1989.

16. Ludlum, *New England Weather Book,* 43–45.

17. Robert H. Simpson and Herbert Riehl, *The Hurricane and Its Impact* (Baton Rouge: Louisiana State Univ. Press, 1981), 289.

18. Popkin, *Environmental Science Services Administration,* 183–84.

19. Roy Leep, phone interview, Aug. 1988.

20. George Winterling, phone interview, Aug. 1988.

21. Dan Rather with Mickey Herskowitz, *The Camera Never Blinks* (New York: William Morrow, 1977), 49.

22. Leslie Raddatz, "Television in the Nation's Service," *TV Guide,* 26 June 1971, 6.

23. Bob Soper, phone interview, 24 Jan. 1989.

24. Raddatz, "Television in the Nation's Service," 6.

25. Patrick J. Michaels, "Weathering the Media Storm," *Washington Post,* 13 Oct. 1985, B-5.

26. Jeff Benkoe, "All Eyes on Mr. Hurricane!" *Washington Post,* 28 Sept. 1985, G-2.

27. Neil Frank, phone interview, 26 Jan. 1989.

28. Bob Case, "The Atlantic Hurricane Season of 1985," *Weatherwise* 39 (1986): 27.

29. Neil Frank, phone interview, 26 Jan. 1989.

30. "Robert Sheets: In the Eye of the Storm," *Commerce People* (Washington: U.S. Department of Commerce, Office of Public Affairs, Feb. 1989), 11.

31. "'Mr. Hurricane' Eyes TV," *USA Today,* 18 Feb. 1987, 2A.

32. Raymond Parr, "83 Dead, 1000 Hurt at Woodward," *Daily Oklahoman,* 11 Apr. 1947, 1.

33. Pat McDermott, "Flash — Tornado Warning!" *Saturday Evening Post,* 28 July 1951, 17–18.

34. McDermott, "Tornado Warning!" 53, 56.

35. Harry Volkman, phone interview, 20 Nov. 1988.

36. Joseph Galway, phone interview, 5 June 1989.

37. Harry Volkman, phone interview, 20 Nov. 1988. (The Raddatz article in *TV Guide* lists the date of WKY's first tornado warning as April 28, 1950, apparently in error.)

38. Dick Smith, "We've Lost Our Picture," *TV Guide,* 1 June 1957, 27.

39. Mogil and Groper, "NWS's Severe Local Storm Programs," 321–22.

40. "Weather Watcher," *Television Age,* 1 Aug. 1966, 46.

41. Raddatz, "Television in the Nation's Service," 8.

42. Ibid.

43. Lloyd Tidwell, "Analyzing the Public Response to Severe Weather Events by Using an Arbitron AID Survey," in *Postprints, 14th Conference on Severe Local Storms* (Boston: American Meteorological Society, 1985), J1.

44. Bob Soper, phone interview, 24 Jan. 1989.

45. H. Michael Mogil, "Weather Emergencies and the Mass Media," in *Postprints, 11th Conference on Severe Local Storms* (Boston: American Meteorological Society, 1979), 562.

46. Blinder, "Stations 'Eye' Storms," 33.

47. Henson, "Comparison of Actual and Perceived Accuracy," 36.

48. William Ritz, "A Case Study of Newspaper Disaster Coverage: The Big Thompson Canyon Flood," in *Disasters and the Mass Media* (Washington: National Academy of Sciences, 1980) 195.

49. "The Society's Awards," BAMS 69 (1988): 924.

Chapter 9. Radio Weather

1. National Oceanic and Atmospheric Administration (NOAA), *Radio and Television Dissemination Issue Study,* May 1981; radio-television file, National Weather Service, Office of Constituent Affairs, Silver Spring, Md., 10.

2. Eric Zorn, "Radio News: Alive and Struggling," *Washington Journalism Review* (Dec. 1987): 18.

3. NOAA, *Radio and Television Dissemination Issue Study,* 11.

4. Ibid.

5. NOAA, *Radio and Television Dissemination Issue Study,* 12.

6. NOAA, *Radio and Television Dissemination Issue Study,* 14.

7. Norm Macdonald, phone interview, 7 July 1989.

8. Don Kent, letter to author, 14 July 1989.

9. "The Society's Awards," BAMS 69 (1988): 923.

10. Jehn, "Radio and Television Weathercasting," 493.

11. Kirk Melhuish, phone interview, 6 July 1989.

12. "Sun or Storm, Listeners Get Coverage to 'Depend On,'" in *Focus* (Atlanta: Cox Enterprises, 1987).

13. Ibid.

14. Kirk Melhuish, phone interview, 6 July 1989.

15. Ibid.

16. *National Weather Digest* 13 (Nov. 1988): 40.

17. Fidler, "Popularizing the Weather," 316.

18. James C. Fidler, "A Weather Program on 500,000 Watts," BAMS 22 (1940): 267–68.

19. "She Does Something About the Weather," *McCall's,* Apr. 1956, 89–90.

20. Peter Leavitt, phone interview, 27 July 1989.

21. Robert A. Mamis, "Forecasting a Profit," *Inc.,* April 1985, 119.

22. Peter Leavitt, phone interview, 27 July 1989.

23. "Television Industry's Commercial Weather Reporting Firm Employs 31 Meteorologists," *P.D. Cue,* June-July 1978, 14.

24. Jim Candor, phone interview, 28 July 1989.

25. Ibid.

26. Joel Myers, phone interview, Dec. 1987.
27. Jim Candor, phone interview, 28 July 1989.
28. "The Weatherman," *Small Market Radio Newsleter,* 24 Mar. 1988, 7–8.
29. Ibid.

Chapter 10 Tomorrow's Outlook

1. Valerie Voss, phone interview, 15 Feb. 1989.
2. John Coleman, phone interview, 28 June 1989.
3. Jay Rosen, "Don't Need a Weatherman?" *Harper's Magazine,* April 1989, 35.
4. Rosen, "Don't Need," 36.

Selected Bibliography

As a field of inquiry, television weather has long been neglected. The vast majority of writing on the subject has appeared in newspapers and magazines; many of these pieces are mere diatribes or superficial surveys. Treatment of television weather in book form is almost nonexistent. Still, much can be gleaned from the material that is available.

The biggest bodies of work on weathercasting are in two publications: *TV Guide* (the popular weekly magazine) and *Bulletin of the American Meteorological Society* (BAMS) (the monthly update for society members). Articles from these two periodicals are listed in separate groups below. Other materials are grouped according to type of publication: consumer or trade magazine, newspaper, scholarly journal, book, or government document.

In selecting materials to be included, I looked for thorough treatments of television weather in general and for in-depth examinations of a specific weathercaster or situation. There are many other newspaper and magazine articles with useful bits of information on television weather; some may be found in the Notes under the relevant chapter. Large selections of such articles are on file at the Broadcast Pioneers Library and the National Association of Broadcasters Library, both in Washington, D.C.

TV Guide

Many *TV Guide* articles are uncredited to an author. Some are editorials under the regular heading "As We See It"; these are listed below with the titles given in the *25 Year Index to TV Guide* (these titles do not appear in the magazine itself). Similarly, titles given below for features are from the *Index* or from tables of contents. Some articles from the *Index* appear only in local *TV Guide* editions and not nationally. These, along with pieces not directly relevant to television weather-casting, have been omitted from the list below.

"As We See It: Chief Job of TV Weathermen Is to Make U.S. Weather Bureau Predictions Interesting." 2 Feb. 1957, inside front cover.
"As We See It: An Improvement in TV Weather Forecasts." 18 July 1959, inside front cover.

"As We See It: Zipping Up Weather Forecasts." 2 Sept. 1961, inside front cover. (Examines the feud between bandleader Guy Lombardo and New York weathercasters, who were accused of driving people away from Lombardo's outdoor concerts with gloomy forecasts.)

"As We See It: Weathermen Should Think Before They Speak." 15 Jan. 1977, A-4. (Recounts the saga of New York's Tex Antoine and the offhand remark about rape that cost him his job.)

"As We See It: Eliminating the Weatherman from Local News Shows." 9 Apr. 1977, A-4. (Discusses the removal of weathercasters from a St. Louis station.)

"Davis, Francis K., Jr. "Weather Is No Laughing Matter." 23 July 1955, 10–11. (Criticism of the mid-1950s gimmicky weathercasts from a meteorologist and pioneer weathercaster. Includes an editorial response to Davis, focusing on "weathergirls.")

Durslag, Melvin. "TV Weathermen." 24 Mar. 1973, 6–9. (A fairly complete and balanced look at TV weather c. 1973.)

"Fair and Wet." 4 Feb. 1956, 12. (Short piece on Ginger Stanley, CBS "Morning Show" weathercaster dunked in a tank on camera.)

Kiester, Edwin Jr. "An Uncanny TV Weatherman." 28 Sept. 1974, 12–15. (Profile of Harry Geise, a private weathercaster in California; focuses more on his long-range forecasting than on his television experience.)

Levin, Eric. "How Television Covers Tornadoes." 3 Aug. 1974, 32–35. (Informative look at coverage of the 1974 tornado outbreak in Cincinnati; Indianapolis; Huntsville, Ala.; and elsewhere.)

_____. "Outlook for Weather Forecasts: Partly Cloudy." 13 May 1978, 16–17. (A typical survey of weathercasting, noting the trend toward severe weather coverage in such cities as Minneapolis and St. Louis.)

_____. "AM Weather: No-Frills Forecasts." 27 March 1982, 44–45. (Examination of the show and its devoted following, with some interesting quotes and anecdotes."

Moore, Frazier. "An Uncertain Forecast for TV's Weather Channel." 1 Jan. 1983, 28–30. (Brief but fact-filled coverage of TWC.)

Moore, Ray. "The Weatherman's Lament." 23 Mar. 1957, 5–7. (Lighthearted piece by a weathercaster at WSB (Atlanta) on how the public sees television weather.)

"Morgus the Weather Ghoul." 21 Nov. 1959, 6–7. (Story and photos of Morgus, a costumed weathercaster at New Orleans' WWL.)

Raddatz, Leslie. "Television in the Nation's Service." 26 June 1971, 6–13. (In-depth survey of television stations' public-service efforts, most relating to weather. The date given in this article for the first tornado warning — April 28, 1950 — was contradicted in interviews for this book.)

Simon, Roger. "TV Weatherpersons Insist on Hamming It Up." 27 May 1989, 12–15. (Standard review of the field.)

Smith, Dick. "We've Lost Our Picture." 1 June 1957, 27. (Tornado coverage on Oklahoma television.)

"Tedi Thurman, Weathergirl Supreme." 19 Oct. 1957, 5–6. (NBC's "Tonight" weathercaster and her approach, which relied on sex appeal.)

"Television Tower with a Forecast." 19 July 1958, 5. (Photo and short piece on the KMTV [Omaha] transmitting tower equipped with multicolored lights that gave a coded forecast.)

Waters, Craig. "Temperatures Will Climb into the Mid-130s. . . ." 22 Apr. 1978, 34–35. (Training of six Saudi Arabian meteorologists in television-weather-casting techniques.)

Bulletin of the American Meteorological Society (BAMS)

While oriented to the professional meteorologist, most of the features below are accessibly written and offer a wealth of detailed information on weathercasting, in many cases from a first-person viewpoint. Entries below are by volume number, year, and page number(s). As with *TV Guide,* some BAMS articles give no author credit. Many issues of BAMS not noted below have short references to television weather as part of regular columns and features. The names of AMS award recipients and seal-of-approval holders are published in BAMS each August.

Bates, F. C. "Severe Local Storm Forecasts and Warnings and the General Public." 43 (1962): 288–91. (An informal overview of the history and problems covering severe storms, particularly tornadoes.)

Beebe, Robert. "TV Weathercaster Ratings — Professional vs. Nonprofessional." 51 (1970): 399–401. (A follow-up to Booker's study, below, this project looks at station pairings in cities nationwide to come up with the same result as Booker: professionals' ratings are higher.)

Booker, D. Ray. "A Comparison of Program Ratings of Professional and Nonprofessional Weathercasters." 43 (1962): 223–28. (This well-thought-out study found ratings substantially higher when weathercasts are delivered by meteorologists.)

Brunk, Ivan. "Improvement on TV Weather Programs." 53 (1972): 1169–72. (A detailed but exceedingly critical evaluation of the verbiage and visuals used in television weather.)

Davis, Francis. "The Professional Meteorologist in Radio." 30 (1949): 86–89. (Davis outlines the emphasis of his programs on WFIL [Philadelphia] and gives samples of viewer comment.)

_____. "Weather and the Media." 57 (1976): 1331–32. (History of early weathercasting and the AMS seal's development.)

Dodson, Eugene. "The Professional Broadcast Meteorologist as Seen by Management." 49 (1968): 366–68. (A meteorologist from WTVT [Tampa] discusses the growth of serious weathercasting.)

Fidler, James C. "Popularizing the Weather Broadcast." 19 (1938): 310–17. (Examines Fidler's early shows on WLBC [Muncie, Ind.] and other radio weather shows in the eastern United States.)

_____. "A Weather Program on 500,000 Watts." 22 (1941), 264–28. (Very detailed look at Fidler's radio broadcasts on WLW [Cincinnati].)

_____. "Weather via Television." 29 (1948): 329–31. (One of the first serious treatments of the potential and problems in doing television weather, as judged from a Weather Bureau experiment.)

_____. "Dial WLW for Weather." 38 (1957): 59–61. (Description of weather coverage on WLW-TV [Cincinnati] and its subsidiary stations in Ohio.)

Hungerford, Arthur. "Opportunities for Meteorologists in Public Broadcasting." 49 (1968): 372–76. (A look at options opened by the Public Broadcasting Act of 1967. Includes a survey of personnel from 19 public television stations on their attitude toward weather broadcasts.)

Jehn, K. H. "The Challenge of Television Weather Programs." 37 (1956): 351–53. (Text of a speech heralding the creation of the AMS seal program.)

_____. "Recognition of Competence in Weathercasting — the AMS Seal of Approval Program." 40 (1959): 85–89. (Formal AMS announcement of the new seal program; includes sample rating form, procedures.)

_____. "Radio and Television Weathercasting—the Seal of Approval Program After Five Years." 45 (1964): 489–93. (Candid examination of the AMS seal program's growth and acceptance.)

King, Jack. "Instrumentation and the Weather Program." 49 (1968): 364–65. (Hints for weathercasters on improving the technical side of their programs.)

Leep, Roy. "The Seal of Approval." 49 (1968): 359–60. (Short subjective comments on the seal program from a television veteran.)

Long, William H. "The Relevance of a University Degree in Meteorology for the Broadcast Meteorologist." 49 (1968): 369–71. (A college professor's informal proposal for a curriculum preparing students for television weathercasting.)

Partridge, Charles Stevens. "As One Weather Fan to Another: The WOR Weather Program." 30 (1949): 29–31. (The radio weathercaster describes his approach at New York's WOR.)

Pearson, Allen D. "Tornado Warnings Over Radio and Television." 49 (1968): 361–63. (From the head of Kansas City's National Severe Storm Forecast Center, the text of a semihumorous speech on the handling and mishandling of tornado warnings in media.)

Ryan, Robert T. "The Weather Is Changing ... or Meteorologists and Broadcasters, the Twain Meet." 63 (1982): 308–10. (Text of a speech by the WRC [Washington] weathercaster summarizing the AMS seal program and forecast problems.)

Stone, R. G. "The Weatherman Eyes Television." 30 (1949): 33–35. (A lively piece on Louie Allen's pioneering weathercasts in Washington, D.C.)

Thomas, Bob. "Meteorology: Science to Show Biz." 53 (1972): 1165–66. (General comments from a television weatherman on his craft.)

Trade Magazines

Applebaum, Simon. "Second Wind." *CableVision Plus,* 14 Nov. 1983, 38–49. (Thorough look at The Weather Channel's first 18 months, focusing on the business end; includes interview with John Coleman.)

Atkins, Bret M. "A TV Meteorologist on Your Radio Station." *RTNDA Communicator,* Dec. 1986, 17.

Becker, Rodney, J., and Edward M. Gross. "National Weather Service Dissemination Systems: Current Modes and Exciting New Possibilities." *RTNDA Communicator,* Dec. 1986, 11–13. (Examines the particulars of accessing NWS data.)

Blinder, Eva J. "Stations 'Eye' Storms with Doppler Radar." *Broadcast Management/Engineering,* Dec. 1985, 33–36. (The use of Doppler on television in New York, Des Moines, and elsewhere.)

Conte, Joseph J. "NOAA Weather Radio, a News Director's Light During the Darkness of Disaster." *RTNDA Communicator,* Aug. 1984, 17–18.

"Format Polish Helps the Weather Channel." *Television/Radio Age,* 10 Nov. 1986, 60.

"Landmark Names Wynne to Head Weather Channel." *Broadcasting,* 22 Aug. 1983, 37–38. (Summary of the contentious power shift at TWC.)

Myers, Barry Lee, and Joel N. Myers. "New Technology and the Presentation of Weather." *RTNDA Communicator,* Dec. 1985, 12–14. (General tips for broadcasters on selecting television-weather graphics systems.)

Myers, Joel N. "Broadcast Meteorology—A Look Ahead at Developments in Weather Graphics, Databases and Delivery Systems of the Near Future."

RTNDA Communicator, Dec. 1987, 24–25. (Update on NWS product changes that affect television weather.)

Paulson, Bob. "Weather Graphics." *RTNDA Communicator,* Dec. 1985, 20–21. (Good overview of the relationships between companies dealing in television-weather graphics.)

Prince, Suzan D. "Weather Mania." *NATPE Programmer,* Sept. 1987, 40–41. (Survey of how various television stations are using computer graphics.)

Root, Steven A. "Automated Weather for Forecasting: A New Tool." *Broadcast Engineering,* Oct. 1981, 68. (An early examination of the computer-graphics trend in television weather, focusing on private meteorological firms.)

Singletary, Michael W. "Weather Reporting." *RTNDA Communicator,* Mar. 1981, 16–17. (Survey of 300 AMS members asking their opinion of their local weathercasters. Most expressed satisfaction with the quality and length of weather segments.)

"Taming a Tornado." *Television Age,* 4 July 1966, 92. (Station WIBW's handling of the severe tornado that struck Topeka, Kansas.)

Trapassc, L. Michael, Randy Bowman, and Laura Daniel. "TV Weather Forecasters." *RTNDA Communicator,* Dec. 1985, 16–18. (Survey of 130 stations on their weather personnel and equipment.)

Veraska, Don. "Fancy Forecasts." *Electronic Media,* 24 Nov. 1986, 34–40. (Weathercasters and news directors comment on the rapid changes in television-weather graphics.)

Wagner, Bill. "Producer's Perspective: When Weather Is the Lead." *RTNDA Communicator,* Dec. 1985, 9.

Other Magazines

"America's Weather Wackies Take Their Forecasting with a Vane of Salt." *People,* 7 Sept. 1981, 24–27. (Short profiles of weathercasters: Willard Scott ["Today"], Harry Wappler [KIRO, Seattle], Don Noe [WPLG, Miami], Kristine Hanson [KCRA, Sacramento], and George Fischbeck [KABC, Los Angeles].)

Blount, Roy, Jr., "Weathercasters: Getting to Snow You." *More,* Apr. 1978, 30–34. (The noted humorist takes a lighthearted look at the 8th Weathercasting Conference of the AMS.)

"Chicago Weatherman Has Resolve for Job Madness." *Jet,* 24 July 1975, 20–22. (The story of Jim Tilmon, one of the country's veteran black weathercasters, at WMAQ, Chicago.)

"Fair-Weather Friends." *Time,* 12 Apr. 1968, 82–83. (Overview of the field. Photos of Tex Antoine, Bill Keene, Don Kent, Frank Field.)

Foster, Phil. "The New England Weather Net." *Weatherwise* 12 (1959): 109–10. (Description of Don Kent's extensive weather-watching network based at WBZ, Boston.)

Garelik, Glenn. "The Weather Peddlers." *Discover,* Apr. 1985, 18–29. (Excellent, well-researched look at weathercasting c. 1985. Perhaps the best popular overview from recent years. Includes many photos.)

Keerdoja, Eileen. "Former Weatherman Leads a Sunny Life." *Newsweek,* 6 June 1983, 12. (The varied careers of John Clinton Youle since he left NBC and weathercasting in 1959.)

Kierein, Tom. "The Hi-Tech World of TV Weathercasting." *Weatherwise* 41 (1988): 150–54. (Kierein [WRC, Washington] documents the work of fellow WRC weathercaster Bob Ryan.)

Morrow, Lance. "The Wonderful Art of Weathercasting." *Time,* 17 Mar. 1980, 61. (Thoughtful, generous essay on the field.)

Naughton, Cliff. "Pre-dawn Patrol." *Professional Pilot,* Mar. 1988, 82–83. (A rare behind-the-scenes depiction of "AM Weather" and its preparation.)

Reed, Mary. "Up on the Roof." *Weatherwise* 41 (1988): 155–56. (An interview with Mike McClellan, a meteorologist at WICS, Springfield, Ill.)

"Reliable Weathercasts." *Science News Letter* 69 (1956): 74. (Brief report on the AMS meeting that mandated a seal-of-approval program.)

Rosen, Jay. "Don't Need a Weatherman?" *Harper's,* Apr. 1989, 34–36. (Incisive thoughts on the future of television weather; condensed from "Coming Next: The Weather as a Political Issue," *Et Cetera,* Spring 1989.)

Teel, Leonard Ray. "The Weather Channel." *Weatherwise* 35 (1982): 156–63. (By far the most in-depth article on The Weather Channel's formation and first few days of operation; many photos.)

"Weather Work for Women." *Life,* 28 Mar. 1955, 8–10. (This picture feature from the height of television weather's most gimmicky period illustrates some of the devices used by both men and women.)

Wiezel, Edwin P. "NOAA Weather Radio." *Weatherwise* 31 (1978): 147–51. (Very detailed article on the government radio network and its enthusiastic acceptance by listeners nationwide.)

"The Wind Rose." *American Weather Observer.* This ongoing irregular feature spotlights television and radio weathercasters. "Wind Rose" subjects have included Tom Stephens (WANE, Fort Wayne, Ind.), Mar. 1984; Bob Ryan (WRC, Washington), Apr. 1984; Dave Lesher (Western Maryland Weather), May 1984; Dick Goddard (WJKN, Cleveland), July 1984; David Apple (KPTV, Portland, Ore.), August 1984; Frank Faulconer (WTVQ, Lexington, Ky.), Sept. 1984; Kerry Kinsey (WABI, Bangor Me.), Mar. 1985; Vince Condella (WITI, Milwaukee), Jan. 1986; Harold Taft (KXAS, Fort Worth), Jan. 1987; Roy Leep (WTVT, Tampa), May 1987; Valerie Voss (CNN), Sept. 1987; Michael Pechner (KRON, San Francisco), Mar. 1988; Frank Cariello (WUAB, Cleveland), Apr. 1988; and Sam Shad (KTVN, Reno), Oct. 1988. (Though only a few paragraphs in length, several of these articles cover peole working in small markets who seldom receive mention in the national press.)

Youle, Clint. "Telecasting the Weather." *Weatherwise* 5 (1952): 14–15. (Youle describes his Chicago weathercasts and viewer reaction to them.)

Young, Mack. "Wayne Cooper, Weatherman." *Weatherwise* 20 (1967): 167. (Profile of a visually impaired radio weathercaster in Lawton, Oklahoma.)

Newspapers

Bell, Brian. "TV's Weather Reporters." *Washington Star Pictorial Magazine,* 14 Nov. 1954, 18–19. (Approaches and backgrounds of Washington weathercasters, including several "weathergirls.")

Carey, Joseph. "Those Weatherstars Stay Cool and Breezy." *New York Daily News,* 12 July 1981, 4–5. (Extensive look at New York weathercasting. Includes a poll of radio and television critics who rate the local weather talent, along with rare background on famous New York weathercasters [Bob Harris, Tex Antoine].)

Gildea, William. "Weathermen: Putting a Freeze on Humor." *Washington Post,* 31 Jan. 1977, C1. (How the 1977 cold wave modified the humorous styles of some Washington weathercasters, including Willard Scott.)

Michaels, Patrick J. "Weathering the Media Storm." *Washington Post,* 13 Oct. 1985, B5. (Review of Gloria's handling by the National Hurricane Center and television weathercasters.)

Millstein, Gilbert. "The Weather Girls Ride Out a Storm." *The New York Times Magazine,* 6 Oct. 1961, 62–68. (Dated but interesting coverage of the late stages of the "weathergirl" era in New York.)

Nordheiemer, Jon. "Chief Hurricane Scout and TV Personality: Neil LaVerne Frank." *New York Times,* 28 Sept. 1985. (One of the many profiles of Frank, written Sept. 26–28, as Hurricane Gloria approached the United States.)

Proctor, Pam. "All They Do Is Talk About the Weather." *Parade,* 7 Sept. 1975, 12–13. (A fairly standard survey of the field, notable in a period when few such overviews were being written. Comments from Willard Scott, Tex Antoine, Sonny Eliot, and others.)

Rosenberg, Howard. "It's Raining Television Weathermen/Comics!" *Los Angeles Times,* 8 July 1985, VI-1. (This plea for sanity in television weather serves as a useful roundup of weathercasters using a comic approach on national television and in Los Angeles.)

Shaw, David. "Weather: Everyone's No. 1 Story." *Los Angeles Times,* 9 March 1981, 1, 3, 22–23. (Unusually detailed survey of television weather. Also covers newspaper treatment of weather. Delves into the philosophy of television-weather approaches.)

Journals (excluding BAMS)

Degregorio, Thomas J. "NOAA Weather Radio Needs Marketing!" *National Weather Digest* 3 (Aug. 1987): 25–28. (A call for more aggressive promotion of NOAA Weather Radio by the government. Good source of background on weather radio. Includes a small survey.)

Driscoll, Dennis M. "A Survey of the Use of National Weather Service Forecasts by Television Weather Forecasters in the United States." *Weather and Forecasting* 1 (1986): 155–63. (This extensive report looks at responses from 300 weathercasters in cities and towns nationwide. Driscoll stratifies the group to see the relation between demographic variables and reliance on NWS forecasts. Most likely to deviate from the NWS were big-city weathercasters with 6–10 years' experience and an AMS seal.)

————. "A Comparison of Temperature and Precipitation Forecasts Issued by Telecasters and the National Weather Service." *Weather and Forecasting* 3 (1988): 285–95. (Expanding on the theme of his previous work, Driscoll compares six months of weathercasts at seven television stations to the respective NWS forecasts. Frequent but minor differences appeared on 12-, 24-, and 36-hour outlooks; only one station used the NWS products without change.)

Gantz, Walter. "Redundancy and Accuracy of Television Station Weather Reports." *Journalism Quarterly* 59 (1982): 440–46. (Gantz examined a month of weathercasts on three Indianapolis television stations, comparing forecasts between stations and to the observed readings. Though stations rarely had identical predictions, deviations were usually small.)

Hyatt, David, Kathy Riley, and Noel Sederstrom. "Recall of Television Weather Reports." *Journalism Quarterly* 55 (1978): 306–10. (This disconcerting study found that viewers retained very little of the information in evening weathercasts. Only half remembered any part of "tomorrow's forecast." Still, most viewers seemed satisfied with television weather as it was.)

Lazalier, Jeffrey A. "A Report on the Results of a Television Weather Survey." *National Weather Digest* 7 (May 1982): 5–9. (Lazalier compiled responses from 186 weathercasters in the country's top 40 television markets. Information on training, facilities, and forecasting methods is presented.)

Martin, Frank P. "Public Response, Action and Means of Reception of National Weather Service Severe Weather Warnings in Northeast Ohio." *National Weather Digest* 2 (Aug. 1977): 2–5. (A survey of 500 students at the University of Akron and Kent State University on their receipt of and reaction to NWS warnings. Television was the dominant source of weather bulletins for 69 percent of respondents, with 50 percent also hearing bulletins on radio.)

Walls, John. "Media Forecasts — Fact or Fiction." *National Weather Digest* 2 (Feb. 1977): 17–19. (Comments on the difficulty in getting National Weather Service information to the public without misinterpretation. Several problems with radio noted (outdated or truncated forecasts, ad-libbed remarks, etc.)

Books and Theses

Baker, John C. "USDA Weather." In *Farm Broadcasting: The First 60 Years.* Ames: Iowa State Univ. Press, 1981. (This four-page chapter of Baker's book focuses on the use of weather reports in agricultural radio broadcasting. Baker covers a wide range of locales, formats, and periods in radio weather.)

Davis, Gerry. "Willard." In *The Today Show: An Anecdotal History.* New York: William Morrow, 1987. (Davis devotes three pages to the weathercaster who brought flamboyance to the staid "Today" set in 1980. Included are a number of quotes from "Today" staffers, along with photos of Willard as Carmen Miranda and Boy George.)

Disasters and the Mass Media: Proceedings of the Committee on Disasters and the Mass Media Workshop. Washington: National Academy of Sciences, 1980. (Several papers from this February 1979 conference bear directly on the relationships among television, the NWS, and community-warning agencies. One report features a survey of the National Association of Broadcasters on stations' severe-weather-warning policies.)

Fang, I. E. "Illustrating Weather News." In *Television News,* 2d ed. New York: Communication Arts, 1972. (From the era before computer graphics, this chapter of a television-production textbook documents some of the ways weathercasts were illustrated before 1980. Photos and instructions are included.)

Henson, Robert. "A Comparison of Actual and Perceived Accuracy of Televised Severe Weather in Oklahoma City." M.A. thesis, University of Oklahoma, 1988. (This study includes an assessment of severe weather bulletins on Oklahoma City television during the spring of 1987. The results are then compared to a survey of 102 Oklahoma City residents who rank stations on expected timeliness and accuracy. Large differences between stations in speed of warning were correctly noted by viewers, but no major accuracy variations appeared.)

Hughes, Patrick. *A Century of Weather Service.* New York: Gordon and Breach, 1970. (Hughes' wide-ranging history of the National Weather Service includes several references to the expanding NWS use of electronic media.)

Lamson, Peggy. *Stay Tuned.* Boston: Godine, 1988. (A small segment of this book on television news looks at the weather segments of Bob Copeland [WCVB, Boston] from a behind-the-scenes perspective.)

Lynott, Bob. *The Weather Tomorrow: Why Can't They Get It Right?* Portland, Ore.: Gadfly Press, 1987. (Written by a veteran weathercaster and meteorologist, this is a detailed critique of what Lynott sees as bureaucracy and conservatism in the NWS. Lynott also takes television weather to task for alleged mindless parroting of the NWS.)

Nelson, Bert Laverne. "The First Fifty Years of Weather Broadcasting." M.S. thesis, University of Utah, 1971. (This comprehensive work is by far the most detailed study of television weather in the precomputer era. Nelson covers most of the major trends and personalities, and includes a large bibliography.)

Rapping, Elayne. "The Real News: Game Cancelled Because of Rain." In *The Looking Glass World of Nonfiction TV*. Boston: South End Press, 1987. (A three-page segment of Rapping's book focuses on television weather from a sociological point of view. Few hard facts, but some interesting insights.)

Rather, Dan. "A Child of the Storm." In *The Camera Never Blinks*. New York: William Morrow, 1977. (Rather devotes ten pages to his groundbreaking coverage of Hurricane Carla in 1961 for KHOU, Houston. Despite some overgeneralizations pertaining to meteorology, Rather's account is readable and informative.)

Stone, Sara Howes. "The Effectiveness of the Broadcast Media in Weather Communications in Lubbock, Texas." M.A. thesis, Texas Tech University, 1975. (Stone surveyed 384 Lubbock County residents on their knowledge of severe weather warnings and their attitudes about such warnings. She found widespread understanding of the symbols used on television to denote severe weather. Over half relied on television for weather warnings.)

Whitnaw, Donald R. *A History of the United States Weather Bureau.* (Of the several Weather Bureau/Weather Service histories that exist, Whitnaw's is the most thorough. The shifts in Bureau use of teletype, radio, and early television are well documented.)

Government Documents

Most of the publications and internal communications of the National Weather Service are stored within the service rather than at the usual government depositories. In researching Chapter 4 ("Television and the Weather Service"), my main source for information on NWS policies regarding radio and television was the NWS Office of Constituent Affairs, located at the National Oceanic and Atmospheric Administration's "Gramex" building in Silver Spring, Maryland. All government documents cited in Chapter 4 are on file in Silver Spring; however, the office is not set up for routine public use of this material. Appointments for research visits should thus be scheduled well in advance.

Index

$38.50